Understanding Buddhism

Buddhism for Beginners, A guide that explores the Key Buddhist teachings and path to Zen, Kama and Enlightenment

DAVID M. EATON

© Copyright 2023 - All rights reserved. The contents of this book may not be reproduced, duplicated or transmitted without direct written permission from the author. Under no circumstances will any legal responsibility or blame be held against the publisher for any reparation, damages, or monetary loss due to the information herein, either directly or indirectly.

Legal Notice: This book is copyright protected. This is only for personal use. You cannot amend, distribute, sell, use, quote or paraphrase any part or the content within this book without the consent of the author.

Disclaimer Notice: Please note the information contained within this document is for educational and entertainment purposes only. Every attempt has been made to provide accurate, up to date and reliable complete information. No warranties of any kind are expressed or implied. Readers acknowledge that the author is not engaging in the rendering of legal, financial, medical or professional advice. The content of this book has been derived from various sources. Please consult a licensed professional before attempting any techniques outlined in this book. By reading this document, the reader agrees that under no circumstances is the author responsible for any losses, direct or indirect, which are incurred as a result of the use of information contained within this document, including, but not limited to, errors, omissions, or inaccuracies.

Contents

Introduction to Buddhism 1

Chapter 1: The Life of the Buddha 5

Chapter 2: The Four Noble Truths 11

Chapter 3: The Eightfold Path in More Detail 19

Chapter 4: Meditation and Mindfulness 27

Chapter 5: Karma and Rebirth 39

Chapter 6: The Three Marks of Existence 49

Chapter 7: Buddhist Ethics and Morality 55

Chapter 8: The Three Jewels of Buddhism 63

Chapter 9: Buddhist Cosmology and Symbolism 71

Chapter 10: Buddhist Scriptures and Texts 81

Chapter 11: Buddhist Festivals and Celebrations 87

Chapter 12: Buddhism in the Modern World 95

Chapter 13: Engaging with Buddhist Communities 103

Chapter 14: Creating Your Own Buddhist Practice 113

Conclusion 121

References 123

Introduction to Buddhism

Buddhism is an ancient spiritual tradition that has captivated hearts and minds for centuries. In this book, we will delve into the basic principles and philosophy of Buddhism, thus developing an understanding of the significance of the Buddha and his teachings. We will also provide an overview of the different branches and traditions within Buddhism, offering a comprehensive introduction to this ancient wisdom.

Whether Buddhism is something you want to learn more about to pursue for yourself or not, learning about world religions allows us to become more open-minded and accepting of everyone around us. There is always something to learn, regardless of whether the underlying beliefs are something you want to follow.

All world religions have their core beliefs and for Buddhists, that is the Four Noble Truths, which provide an understanding of the human condition and offer a transformative path toward inner peace and freedom. We will explore these truths in depth, examining the nature of suffering, its causes, and the path to liberation.

Beyond the Four Noble Truths, Buddhism encompasses a rich philosophical framework that addresses fundamental questions about existence, consciousness, and the nature of reality. Concepts such as impermanence, interdependence, and selflessness play a crucial role in shaping the Buddhist worldview. We will explore these concepts, unraveling their implications and practical applications in our lives. By understanding these principles, we gain insight into the nature of our own experiences and the interconnectedness of all beings.

At the heart of Buddhism lies the figure of the Buddha, or Siddhartha Gautama, who achieved enlightenment and became the Awakened One. The Buddha's teachings, known as the Dharma, hold immense significance as they offer a path to liberation from suffering. Through his profound compassion and dedication, the Buddha's teachings continue to inspire and guide millions of people around the world, whether Buddhist or not.

The significance of the Buddha goes beyond his historical role as a spiritual teacher. He represents the embodiment of human potential, demonstrating that enlightenment and liberation are attainable for all beings. The story of his life serves as an inspiration, reminding us that we too can embark on a transformative journey toward self-discovery and liberation. By understanding the significance of the Buddha, we open ourselves to the possibility of tapping into our own innate wisdom and compassion, realizing our true nature.

Overview of the Different Branches and Traditions Within Buddhism

Like all world religions, Buddhism has evolved and diversified over time, giving rise to various branches and traditions. From Theravada, which emphasizes the original teachings of the Buddha, to Mahayana, which focuses on compassion and the pursuit of enlightenment for the benefit of all, each branch offers unique insights and approaches to spiritual growth.

By gaining familiarity with the different branches and traditions, you will be empowered to explore Buddhist practices and find resonance with the path that aligns with your own spiritual journey.

Throughout this book, we will embark on a comprehensive exploration of Buddhism, delving into its teachings, practices, and wisdom. We will examine the core principles that underpin this ancient tradition, providing you with the tools and insights to cultivate inner peace, compassion, and liberation from suffering.

By embracing the wisdom of Buddhism, we open ourselves to a transformative journey of self-discovery, spiritual growth, and the realization of our highest potential.

So, let us embark on this transformative journey together, as we uncover the timeless wisdom of Buddhism and discover the potential it holds for personal growth, spiritual awakening, and a more compassionate world.

Chapter 1

The Life of the Buddha

To truly understand the life and teachings of Siddhartha Gautama, we need to go back in time to gain some historical context and learn more about who he was.

Siddhartha was born around the 6th century BCE into a noble family in ancient India, in the region that is now known as Nepal. This was a time of great intellectual and spiritual development in the Indian subcontinent, with various philosophical and religious traditions flourishing.

Siddhartha's early life was marked by privilege and luxury. He was raised in opulence, shielded from the harsh realities of the world. However, his upbringing did not protect him from the existential questions that arise in the face of human suffering around the world, something which Siddhartha was deeply troubled by.

Motivated by a profound sense of compassion and a burning desire to understand the nature of existence, Siddhartha embarked on a spiritual quest. At the age of 29, he made a momentous decision to renounce his princely life, leaving behind his family, wealth, and all worldly attachments. This act was a radical departure from societal expectations, as he sought a deeper truth beyond the confines of material wealth and social status.

For the next six years, Siddhartha immersed himself in the ascetic practices prevalent in ancient India at the time. He sought out renowned spiritual teachers and engaged in rigorous self-mortification, believing that extreme renunciation of worldly pleasures would lead to enlightenment. However, he soon realized that these extreme practices did not provide the answers he was looking for. Despite subjecting himself to severe physical challenges, he found himself no closer to understanding the nature of suffering and how to stop it.

Realizing his limitations, Siddhartha abandoned these practices and adopted a middle way, a balanced approach between self-indulgence and self-mortification.

The historical context and early life of Siddhartha Gautama provide a backdrop for understanding the transformative journey he undertook. His decision to give up his privileged life and seek answers was a radical departure from societal norms. It reflects the universal human quest for meaning and understanding in the face of life's difficult challenges.

Siddhartha's journey serves as an inspiration to seekers of truth and wisdom. It reminds us that the path to enlightenment is not limited to a specific background or circumstance. It resonates with our own yearning for deeper understanding and liberation from suffering.

The Journey of the Buddha Toward Enlightenment

The Buddha's journey is a beautiful and inspiring tale that encapsulates the human quest for truth, liberation, and inner peace. Siddhartha Gautama embarked on a transformative path that would forever change the course of his life and the lives of countless others.

Leaving behind his family, wealth, and all worldly attachments, Siddhartha ventured into the unknown, seeking answers to the questions that plagued his mind.

Once he realized that extreme practices of self-mortification would not work, Siddhartha turned his attention to deep meditation, seeking direct insight into the nature of reality and the causes of suffering. He sought solitude and seclusion, retreating to forests, caves, and other remote places to engage in intensive meditation practices. With unwavering determination and a steadfast commitment, he delved into the depths of his own mind, exploring the nature of consciousness and the workings of the human experience.

It was during this period of intense introspection that Siddhartha made a momentous decision. He chose to sit beneath the Bodhi tree in Bodh Gaya, India, and vowed not to move until he attained enlightenment. With resolute determination, he faced the inner challenges and obstacles that arose, confronting the depths of his own mind and the illusions that clouded his understanding.

After a night of contemplation and inner struggle, Siddhartha finally achieved his goal. He experienced an awakening, gaining deep insights into the nature of suffering, its causes, and the path to liberation. In that moment, Siddhartha became the Buddha, the Awakened One, and his life's purpose shifted toward sharing his newfound wisdom with others.

The Buddha's journey serves as a timeless reminder of the human capacity for transformation and awakening. It demonstrates that the path to enlightenment is not a straight line, but a process of exploration, self-discovery, and overcoming obstacles. Siddhartha's journey reflects the universal human quest for truth, liberation, and inner peace, inspiring generations to embark on their own spiritual journeys.

Key Events and Teachings During the Buddha's Life

The life of the Buddha was marked by significant events and heartfelt teachings that continue to shape the path of Buddhism. These key events and teachings provide valuable insights into the Buddha's journey and the wisdom he shared with humanity.

Let's look at an overall timeline and explore some of the pivotal moments and teachings that have had a lasting impact on the development of Buddhism.

- **Birth and Early Life:** Siddhartha Gautama was born into a noble family in Lumbini, present-day Nepal. His birth was accompanied by auspicious signs and prophecies, foretelling his future greatness. Despite his privileged upbringing, Siddhartha was deeply moved by the suffering he witnessed in the world, planting the seeds for his spiritual quest.

- **Renunciation:** One of the most significant events in the Buddha's life was his renunciation of worldly life. At the age of 29, he made the courageous decision to leave behind his family, wealth, and all attachments in search of truth and liberation from suffering. This act of renunciation marked the beginning of his spiritual journey.

- **Enlightenment:** After years of intense spiritual practice and deep meditation, Siddhartha attained enlightenment under the Bodhi tree in Bodh Gaya, India. This profound awakening marked a pivotal moment in his life, as he gained deep insights into the nature of suffering, its causes, and the path to liberation.

- **First Sermon:** Following his enlightenment, the Buddha delivered his first sermon, known as the Dhammacakkappavattana Sutta, or the "Turning of the Wheel of Dharma." In this sermon, he shared the Four Noble Truths and introduced the Eightfold Path, providing a comprehensive framework for understanding and transcending suffering. This sermon marked the beginning of his teaching mission.

- **Formation of the Sangha:** The Buddha established a monastic community known as the Sangha, consisting of ordained monks and nuns. This community provided support, guidance, and a framework for spiritual practice. The Sangha played a crucial role in preserving and spreading the Buddha's teachings throughout his lifetime and beyond.

- **Ethical Teachings:** The Buddha emphasized the importance of ethical conduct as a foundation for spiritual growth. He taught the Five Precepts, which are guidelines for moral behavior, including refraining from harming living beings, stealing, engaging in sexual misconduct, lying, and consuming intoxicating substances. Ethical conduct was seen as a crucial aspect of the path towards liberation.

- **Teachings on Meditation:** Meditation held a central place in the Buddha's teachings. He taught various meditation techniques, including mindfulness of breath, loving-kindness meditation, and insight meditation. Meditation was seen as a means to cultivate mindfulness, concentration, and insight, leading to a deep understanding of the nature of reality.

- **Teachings on Impermanence and Non-Self:** The Buddha focused on the concepts of impermanence (anicca) and non-self (anatta). He taught that all things are impermanent and subject to change, and that there is no permanent, unchanging self or soul. These teachings challenged the notion of a fixed and independent self, inviting followers to investigate the nature of their own experiences.

- **Teachings on Compassion and Loving-Kindness:** The Buddha emphasized the cultivation of compassion and loving-kindness toward all beings. He taught that genuine compassion arises from the understanding of the interconnectedness of all life. Practicing compassion and loving-kindness was seen as a means to overcome self-centeredness and develop a deep sense of empathy and care for others.

- **Parinirvana:** The Buddha's physical death, known as Parinirvana, marked the end of his earthly journey. He passed away at the age of 80 in Kushinagar, India. Before his passing, the Buddha imparted his final teachings, emphasizing the importance of individual effort and personal liberation. His teachings and the Sangha continued to thrive after his death, carrying his legacy forward.

These key events and teachings during the Buddha's life provide a glimpse into the transformative journey he undertook and the profound wisdom he shared with humanity. They form the foundation of Buddhism, guiding followers on the path toward liberation from suffering and the realization of ultimate truth.

By studying and embodying these teachings, followers can cultivate wisdom, compassion, and inner peace, following in the noble footsteps of the Buddha.

Chapter 2

The Four Noble Truths

The fundamental teachings of the Buddha form the cornerstone of Buddhism, offering profound insights into the nature of existence, the causes of suffering, and the path to liberation. These teachings, known as the Dharma, provide a comprehensive framework for understanding and transcending suffering.

In this chapter, let's explore the fundamental teachings of the Buddha in depth, gaining a deeper understanding of their significance and practical application in our lives.

The Four Noble Truths

The Four Noble Truths serve as the foundation of the Buddha's teachings. They acknowledge the existence of suffering (dukkha) as an inherent part of human existence. The First Noble Truth recognizes the reality of suffering in various forms, including physical pain, emotional distress, and the unsatisfactory nature of worldly experiences.

The Second Noble Truth delves into the causes of suffering, highlighting the role of craving and attachment. It teaches that our desires and attachments to transient things and experiences lead to suffering. The Third Noble Truth offers hope by proclaiming that the end of suffering is attainable. It emphasizes that liberation from suffering is possible through a lack of craving and attachment.

The Fourth Noble Truth outlines the Eightfold Path, which provides a practical guide for overcoming suffering and gaining liberation.

The Eightfold Path

The Eightfold Path is the path to liberation and enlightenment. It encompasses eight interconnected aspects: Right Understanding, Right Intention, Right Speech, Right Action, Right Livelihood, Right Effort, Right Mindfulness, and Right Concentration. Each aspect represents a key component of ethical conduct, mental discipline, and wisdom.

Right Understanding involves developing a deep understanding of the Four Noble Truths and the nature of reality. Right Intention involves wholesome intentions and moving away from harmful desires. Right Speech emphasizes truthful, kind, and beneficial communication. Right Action encourages ethical behavior and refraining from harming others.

Right Livelihood involves living in an ethical way that supports the path of awakening. Right Effort emphasizes the development of wholesome qualities and the abandonment of unwholesome ones. Right Mindfulness involves developing present-moment awareness and mindfulness in all activities. Right Concentration involves focused and concentrated states of mind through meditation.

Dependent Origination

Dependent Origination (pratītyasamutpāda) is a profound teaching that explains the interdependent nature of all things. It states that everything depends on multiple causes and conditions. According to this teaching, there is no independent, permanent self or soul. Instead, our experiences and identities are shaped by a complex web of causes and conditions.

Understanding dependent origination helps us see the interconnectedness of all beings and the impermanent nature of existence. It invites us to investigate the causes and conditions that give rise to suffering and to cultivate the causes and conditions that lead to liberation.

Impermanence and Non-Self

Buddhism teaches that all things are impermanent (anicca) and subject to change. Nothing in the world remains fixed or unchanging. This teaching emphasizes the concept of non-self (anatta), which suggests that there is no fixed, independent self or essence.

It asks us to investigate our own experiences and to recognize the impermanent and ever-changing nature of ourselves and the world around us. It encourages us to let go of attachments and to develop a deeper understanding of reality.

Mindfulness and Meditation

Mindfulness (sati) and meditation play a central role in the Buddha's teachings. Mindfulness involves being fully present and aware of our thoughts, feelings, and sensations in the present moment. It cultivates a deep sense of self-awareness and helps us break free from the cycle of reactive patterns and automatic behaviors.

Meditation, in various forms, allows us to develop concentration, insight, and a direct experience of reality. It leads to calmness, clarity, and wisdom, and a deeper understanding of ourselves and the nature of existence.

These teachings offer practical guidance for ethical conduct, mental cultivation, and the development of wisdom. By incorporating these teachings into our lives, we can cultivate mindfulness, compassion, and insight, leading to personal growth and spiritual awakening.

However, it's important to note that understanding the Buddha's teachings is just the beginning of the story. The true essence lies in using them. It is through personal practice, reflection, and direct experience that we can truly embody the wisdom of the Buddha's teachings and transform our lives.

Exploring the Nature of Suffering and Its Causes

The Buddha taught that suffering is not limited to physical pain or extreme forms of distress. It encompasses a broader sense of dissatisfaction that invades our lives. It includes the transient nature of pleasure, the experience of dissatisfaction even in moments of apparent happiness, and the angst that arises from the impermanence and uncertainty of life. The Buddha recognized that suffering is an inherent part of the human condition, affecting all of us to varying degrees.

The causes of suffering, according to the Buddha's teachings, can be traced back to three primary roots: craving (tanha), ignorance (avijja), and attachment (upadana).

Craving refers to the insatiable desire for pleasure, possessions, and experiences. It is the relentless pursuit of sensory gratification and the clinging to pleasurable experiences, which ultimately leads to disappointment and dissatisfaction. Ignorance refers to a lack of understanding of the true nature of reality, including the impermanence and interconnectedness of all things. It is the mistaken belief in a fixed and independent self, leading to a distorted perception of ourselves and the world.

Attachment refers to the clinging and grasping onto transient things, experiences, and identities, believing that they can provide lasting happiness and security. This attachment leads to suffering when these things inevitably change or are lost.

The Buddha taught that the root cause of suffering lies in our attachment to the illusion of a permanent and separate self. This attachment creates a sense of separation, leading to desires, aversions, and encourages the cycle of suffering. The belief in a fixed and independent self-causes an illusion of control and ownership, and we suffer when things do not go according to our desires or expectations. The Buddha emphasized that the self is not a fixed entity but a constantly changing process, interdependent with all other phenomena in the universe.

Understanding the nature of suffering and its causes is not just an intellectual exercise but a deeply personal and experiential exploration. The Buddha encouraged followers to investigate their own experiences and to observe the coming and going of sensations, thoughts, and emotions.

The path to the end of suffering involves developing wisdom, ethical conduct, and mental discipline. It begins with Right Understanding, which involves recognizing the nature of suffering, its causes, and the path to its end. Right Understanding is complemented by Right Intention, which involves cultivating wholesome intentions and giving up harmful desires. Ethical conduct, encompassing Right Speech, Right Action, and Right Livelihood, provides a foundation for harmonious relationships and the avoidance of actions that cause harm to us and others.

Mental discipline is achieved through the practice of Right Effort, Right Mindfulness, and Right Concentration. Right Effort involves wholesome qualities and avoiding unwholesome ones. Right Mindfulness involves developing present-moment awareness and mindfulness in all activities, allowing for a direct experience of reality. Finally, Right Concentration involves cultivating focused and concentrated states of mind through meditation, leading to deep insight and liberation from suffering.

Exploring the nature of suffering and its causes is a transformative journey that invites us to examine our own experiences and patterns of attachment. It challenges us to question our deeply ingrained beliefs and to cultivate a deeper understanding of ourselves and the world.

The Buddha's teachings offer a roadmap for understanding and transcending suffering. Through personal practice, reflection, and direct experience, we can gradually alleviate suffering and embark on the path towards liberation and enlightenment.

Introduction to the Concept of Liberation from Suffering

The concept of liberation from suffering lies at the core of Buddhism, offering a transformative path toward freedom, inner peace, and ultimate awakening. It is a profound and fundamental principle that underpins the teachings of the Buddha.

Liberation from suffering is not just an abstract idea but a practical and attainable goal that we can all strive for in our lives.

In Buddhism, suffering is understood as a universal experience that occurs when we are dissatisfied in our worldly existence. It encompasses not only physical pain but also the mental and emotional challenges that we all face.

The concept of liberation from suffering offers a radical shift in perspective. It suggests that suffering is not an inevitable and permanent state, but rather a condition that can be understood, transformed, and ultimately transcended. It is an invitation to explore the nature of suffering, its causes, and the possibility of liberation.

Liberation from suffering involves recognizing and addressing its root causes. To attain liberation from suffering, we must cultivate wisdom, ethical conduct, and mental discipline. Wisdom involves developing a deep understanding of the nature of suffering, its causes, and how to stop it. Ethical conduct encompasses living in alignment with principles of compassion, kindness, and non-harming. Mental discipline involves training the mind through practices such as meditation, mindfulness, and concentration.

By following the Eightfold Path, we can gradually alleviate suffering and cultivate inner peace. It is important to note that liberation from suffering is not a one-time event but an ongoing process of self-discovery and transformation. It requires personal exploration, self-reflection, and the development of mindfulness and awareness.

The concept of liberation from suffering is a central tenet of Buddhism. By exploring the nature of suffering, its causes, and the practical steps outlined in the Eightfold Path, we can embark on a journey of self-discovery, liberation, and the realization of our highest potential.

CHAPTER 3

The Eightfold Path in More Detail

The path to liberation and enlightenment, as taught by the Buddha, is known as the Eightfold Path. It consists of eight interconnected aspects that provide a comprehensive framework for spiritual growth and the alleviation of suffering.

We've introduced these briefly, but in this chapter, we're going to delve more deeply into what they mean and how you can introduce them into your life. As a reminder, they are: Right Understanding, Right Intention, Right Speech, Right Action, Right Livelihood, Right Effort, Right Mindfulness, and Right Concentration.

These eight aspects of the Eightfold Path are not steps to be followed in a straight line or set sequence. Instead, they are interconnected and support one another, forming a holistic approach to spiritual development. Each aspect contributes to the cultivation of wisdom, ethical conduct, and mental discipline, leading to the alleviation of suffering and the realization of our true nature.

The practice of meditation plays a central role in the path to liberation and enlightenment. Through meditation, we can cultivate mindfulness, concentration, and insight. Meditation allows for the cultivation of a calm and focused mind, leading to clarity, wisdom, and the direct experience of reality.

Alongside that, mindfulness is a key component of the path. It involves being fully present and aware in each moment, cultivating a non-judgmental and accepting attitude toward our experiences. It allows us to observe our thoughts, emotions, and sensations without getting entangled in them, and provides a foundation for developing insight into the nature of reality and the causes of suffering.

But of course, this path is not without its challenges. It requires confronting and transforming deeply ingrained patterns of attachment, aversion, and ignorance. It involves letting go of deeply held beliefs and identities that cause suffering. It requires facing the impermanence and uncertainty of life with bravery and wisdom.

Understanding the Eight Steps/Paths of Ethical Conduct, Meditation, and Wisdom

The eight steps provide a comprehensive framework for us to navigate our spiritual journey and cultivate inner peace, compassion, and insight. In this section, we'll explore each step in detail, understanding their significance and practical application in our lives.

Right Understanding

Right Understanding involves developing a deep understanding of the nature of suffering, its causes, and the path to the end of pain. It is the foundation upon which the entire path is built. Right Understanding includes recognizing the impermanence and interconnectedness of all things, understanding the law of cause and effect (karma), and gaining insight into the nature of reality.

It is through Right Understanding that we can develop a clear and accurate view of ourselves and the world.

Right Intention

Right Intention involves cultivating wholesome intentions and giving up harmful desires. It is about aligning our intentions with the principles of compassion, kindness, and non-harming. Right Intention encourages us to let go of ill-will, greed, and harmful intentions, and instead cultivate intentions rooted in goodwill, generosity, and wisdom.

Right Intention allows us to set the direction for our thoughts, words, and actions.

Right Speech

Right Speech emphasizes truthful, kind, and beneficial communication. It involves avoiding lying, divisive and harsh speech, and idle gossip. Right Speech encourages us to use our words to promote harmony, understanding, and compassion.

Right Speech pushes us to cultivate integrity, build positive relationships, and contribute to a more harmonious society.

Right Action

Right Action involves ethical behavior and refraining from actions that cause harm to us and others. It encompasses refraining from killing, stealing, and engaging in sexual misconduct. Right Action encourages us to act with integrity, respect for life, and consideration for the well-being of others.

It is through Right Action that we can cultivate a sense of responsibility and contribute to a more compassionate and just world.

Right Livelihood

Right Livelihood involves engaging in a life that is ethical and supports the path of awakening. It encourages us to choose a vocation that does not cause harm in any way. Right Livelihood emphasizes the importance of integrity, honesty, and the avoidance of professions that involve exploitation, violence, or unethical practices.

Right Livelihood encourages us to align our work with our spiritual values and contribute positively to society.

Right Effort

Right Effort involves making a sustained effort to cultivate wholesome qualities and abandon unwholesome ones. It is about actively developing positive qualities such as generosity, loving-kindness, and wisdom, while letting go of negative ones such as greed, hatred, and delusion. Right Effort pushes us to develop a balanced and diligent approach to our spiritual practice.

Right Effort helps us to cultivate inner strength, resilience, and the ability to overcome obstacles.

Right Mindfulness

Right Mindfulness is the practice of being fully present and aware of our thoughts, feelings, bodily sensations, and our surrounding environment, developing a non-judgmental and accepting awareness of the present moment. Right Mindfulness allows us to observe our experiences without getting too caught up in them.

It provides a foundation for developing insight into the nature of reality and the causes of suffering. Through Right Mindfulness, we achieve clarity, concentration, and a deep understanding of ourselves and the world.

Right Concentration

Right Concentration involves developing a focused and concentrated state of mind through meditation. Then, we can cultivate a deep state of tranquility and stability. Right Concentration is achieved through various meditation practices, such as mindfulness of breath, loving-kindness meditation, and insight meditation. It leads to the deepening of insight, the purification of the mind, and the direct experience of reality.

Through Right Concentration, we achieve a calm and focused mind, free from distractions and hindrances.

The Eightfold Path is a combination of steps that are interconnected and mutually supportive, guiding us on a transformative journey toward liberation and enlightenment. By integrating these steps into our lives, we can cultivate inner peace, compassion, and insight, leading to personal growth and spiritual awakening.

Practical Tips for Incorporating the Eightfold Path Into Your Daily Life

As we previously mentioned, The Eightfold Path is a fundamental concept in Buddhism that provides guidance on how to live a meaningful and fulfilling life. It consists of eight interconnected principles that, when practiced diligently, can lead to the end of suffering and the attainment of enlightenment.

While the Eightfold Path may seem daunting at first, it is important to remember that it is a lifelong journey of self-discovery and personal growth. Here are some practical tips for incorporating the Eightfold Path into your daily life:

Right Understanding

To implement Right Understanding into your life, you should study and reflect upon the teachings of Buddhism. This can be done through reading books, attending lectures, or engaging in discussions with fellow practitioners.

Additionally, it is important to question your own beliefs and assumptions and be open to new perspectives.

Right Intention

Start by setting clear and positive intentions for your day. This could be as simple as intending to be kind and compassionate towards others, or to approach challenges with patience and equanimity. Regularly reflect on your intentions and make adjustments as needed.

Right Speech

Right Speech emphasizes the importance of using words that are truthful, kind, and beneficial. To do this, practice mindful speech by pausing before speaking and considering the impact of your words. Avoid gossip, harsh language, and divisive speech. Instead, strive to communicate with honesty, empathy, and respect.

Right Action

To implement Right Action into your life, treat all living beings with kindness and compassion, and practice generosity by offering help and support to those in need. Avoid actions that cause harm, such as stealing, lying, or engaging in harmful relationships. Cultivate mindfulness in your actions and strive to make choices that align with your values.

Right Livelihood

Choose a profession or occupation that aligns with your values and contributes positively to society. Avoid engaging in activities that cause harm or exploit others, and regularly reflect on the impact of your work, making adjustments as necessary.

Right Effort

To bring Right Effort into your life, practice mindfulness and self-awareness to recognize unwholesome thoughts, emotions, and behaviors. Then, make a conscious effort to replace them with wholesome alternatives. This may involve cultivating qualities such as kindness, patience, and generosity.

Remember to regularly reflect on your progress and celebrate small victories.

Right Mindfulness

Right Mindfulness is the practice of being fully present and aware in the present moment. You can achieve this through formal meditation practices, such as sitting or walking meditation. You can also bring mindfulness into your daily activities by paying attention to your senses, thoughts, and emotions. Regularly check in with yourself and observe your experiences without judgment.

Right Concentration

Cultivate concentration through meditation practices that involve focusing on a single object, such as the breath or a mantra. Regularly set aside time for formal meditation practice to strengthen your concentration. Additionally, seek opportunities to cultivate concentration in your daily life, such as during work or leisure activities.

Incorporating the Eightfold Path into daily life requires consistent effort and practice. Start by focusing on one aspect of the path at a time and gradually incorporate others as you progress. Remember that the path is not about perfection, but about continuous growth and learning. Be patient with yourself and celebrate small victories along the way.

You may find it helpful to surround yourself with like-minded people who can support and inspire you. Look for local Buddhist groups or online forums where you can connect with others on the same journey. Engaging in discussions, sharing experiences, and learning from others can greatly enhance your understanding and practice of the Eightfold Path.

Remember that the Eightfold Path is not meant to be a rigid set of rules, but rather a flexible framework that can be adapted to your own unique circumstances and personality. It is a guide to help you navigate the complexities of life and cultivate inner peace and wisdom.

By incorporating the principles of the Eightfold Path into your daily life, you can gradually transform your thoughts, words, and actions, leading to a more compassionate, mindful, and fulfilling existence. Embrace the journey, be kind to yourself, and enjoy the transformative power of the Eightfold Path.

Chapter 4

Meditation and Mindfulness

Meditation is a central practice in Buddhism, and a powerful tool for cultivating mindfulness, concentration, and insight. It is an ancient practice that has been passed down through generations, and it continues to be a cornerstone of Buddhist teachings and traditions.

In this chapter, let's explore the practice of meditation in Buddhism, its benefits, and how to incorporate it into your own spiritual journey.

The Purpose and Types of Meditation in Buddhism

In Buddhism, meditation serves as a means to develop a deep understanding of the nature of reality as well as to cultivate inner peace and wisdom. Through meditation, we can directly experience the impermanent, unsatisfactory, and selfless nature of existence, as taught in the Three Marks of Existence.

Meditation is seen as a path to liberation from suffering and the achievement of enlightenment. By training the mind to be present and focused, we can develop insight into the true nature of reality and transcend the cycle of birth, death, and rebirth.

There are various types of meditation practiced in Buddhism, each with its own unique focus and technique. Some of the most common ones include:

- **Samatha (Calm Abiding) Meditation:** This form of meditation aims to cultivate tranquility and concentration. The aim is to focus on a single object, such as breath, a mantra, or a visual image, in order to calm the mind and develop deep concentration.

- **Vipassana (Insight) Meditation:** Vipassana meditation involves the cultivation of insight and wisdom. Here, we observe the ebb and flow of thoughts, sensations, and emotions without attachment or judgment. This practice allows for a direct experience of the impermanent and selfless nature of everything around us.

- **Metta (Loving-Kindness) Meditation:** Metta meditation involves the cultivation of unconditional love, compassion, and goodwill toward us and others. This type involves the repetition of phrases and visualizing sending loving-kindness to ourselves, loved ones, unknown, and even difficult people. Metta meditation helps to develop a heart of compassion and overcome negative emotions.

- **Walking Meditation:** Walking meditation is a form of meditation that involves slow, mindful walking. When doing this, we focus our attention on the sensations of walking, such as the movement of our feet and their contact with the ground. This type of meditation can be particularly helpful for those who find it challenging to sit still for extended periods.

The Benefits of Meditation in Buddhism

Meditation offers numerous benefits for both the mind and body. Some of the key benefits include:

- **Cultivating Mindfulness:** Meditation helps to develop mindfulness, which is the ability to be fully aware in the present moment. This heightened awareness allows us to observe our thoughts, emotions, and sensations without judgment, leading to a greater understanding of the mind and the ability to respond positively to life's challenges.

- **Developing Concentration:** Through regular meditation practice, we can strengthen our concentration and focus. This can be applied to various aspects of life, such as work, study, and daily activities, leading to increased productivity and effectiveness.

- **Reducing Stress and Anxiety:** Meditation has been shown to reduce stress and anxiety by activating the body's relaxation response. By calming the mind and body, we experience a sense of inner peace and tranquility.

- **Cultivating Compassion and Empathy:** Practices such as loving-kindness meditation help to develop compassion, empathy, and kindness toward ourselves and others. This leads to improved relationships, greater emotional well-being, and a more harmonious society.

Incorporating Meditation into Your Life

If you are interested in incorporating meditation into your own spiritual journey, here are some practical tips to get started:

- **Start with Short Sessions:** Begin with short meditation sessions, such as 5-10 minutes, and gradually increase the time spent as you become more comfortable. Consistency is more important than time, so aim for regular practice rather than long sessions.

- **Find a Quiet Space:** Choose a quiet and peaceful space where you can meditate without distractions. Create a comfortable environment with a cushion or chair and ensure that you sit in a way that allows for alertness and relaxation.

- **Focus on Your Breath:** A simple and effective meditation object is your breath. Direct your attention to the sensation of your breath entering and leaving your body. Whenever your mind wanders, gently bring it back to your breath without judgment.

- **Be Gentle with Yourself:** Meditation is a practice of non-judgment and self-compassion. Be patient with yourself and let go of any expectations or judgments that may arise. Treat yourself with kindness and understanding as you navigate the ups and downs of your new endeavor.

- **Explore Guided Meditations:** If you find it helpful, explore guided meditations led by experienced teachers. These can provide structure and guidance, especially for beginners. There are numerous resources available online, including apps, websites, and podcasts.

- **Integrate Mindfulness Into Your Daily Life:** Extend the benefits of meditation into your daily life by practicing mindfulness in everyday activities. Pay attention to the present moment as you eat, walk, or engage in conversations. This helps to cultivate a sense of presence and awareness throughout the day.

Meditation is a personal journey, and it is important to find a practice that resonates with you. Experiment with different techniques and approaches and trust your own experience. Remember, you may not master meditation overnight, but the more you persist, the easier it will become.

Understanding Different Meditation Techniques and Their Benefits

Meditation is a practice that has been embraced by various cultures and spiritual traditions for centuries. There are countless different techniques, each with its own unique focus and benefits. Whether you are a beginner, or you've meditated before, understanding different techniques can help you find the approach that resonates with you and supports your personal growth and well-being.

Let's explore some different types.

Mindfulness Meditation

Mindfulness meditation is a technique that involves bringing our attention to the present moment with non-judgmental awareness. It is often practiced by focusing on the breath, bodily sensations, or the environment. The benefits of mindfulness meditation include:

- **Stress Reduction**: Mindfulness meditation helps to cultivate a state of calm and relaxation, reducing stress and anxiety.

- **Improved Focus and Concentration**: Regular practice enhances attention and concentration, allowing for greater productivity and mental clarity.

- **Emotional Regulation**: Mindfulness meditation helps to develop emotional intelligence, allowing us to observe and respond to emotions with greater awareness.

- **Increased Self-Awareness**: By cultivating present-moment awareness, mindfulness meditation enables us to gain deeper insights into our thoughts, emotions, and behaviors.

Loving-Kindness Meditation

Loving-kindness meditation, also known as metta meditation, involves developing feelings of love, compassion, and goodwill towards ourselves and others. It typically involves silently repeating phrases or visualizing sending loving-kindness to different people or groups.

The benefits of loving-kindness meditation include:

- **Enhanced Compassion**: Regular practice of loving-kindness meditation helps to develop a sense of empathy and compassion towards ourselves and others.

- **Improved Relationships**: By cultivating loving-kindness, we experience greater connection and understanding in our relationships, leading to improved communication and harmony.

- **Reduced Hostility and Anger**: Loving-kindness meditation helps to soften negative emotions, such as anger and hostility, and promotes forgiveness and understanding.

- **Increased Well-Being**: Practicing loving-kindness meditation has been shown to increase positive emotions, overall well-being, and life satisfaction.

Transcendental Meditation

Transcendental Meditation (TM) is a technique that involves the use of a mantra, a specific sound or phrase, to achieve a state of deep relaxation and inner peace. TM is typically practiced for 15-20 minutes, twice a day. The benefits of transcendental meditation include:

- **Stress Reduction**: TM promotes deep relaxation, reducing stress and anxiety.

- **Improved Brain Function**: Research suggests that TM enhances brain function, including increased creativity, improved memory, and enhanced cognitive abilities.

- **Enhanced Self-Actualization**: TM is believed to support personal growth and self-actualization, leading to greater self-confidence and fulfillment.

- **Increased Resilience**: Regular practice of TM helps us develop resilience and the ability to bounce back from challenges.

Breath Awareness Meditation

Breath awareness meditation involves focusing attention on our breath, observing its natural rhythm and sensations. This technique is simple yet powerful, and it can be practiced anywhere, anytime. The benefits of breath awareness meditation include:

- **Stress Reduction**: Focusing on our breath helps to calm the mind and relax the body, reducing stress and promoting a sense of well-being.

- **Improved Concentration**: Breath awareness meditation enhances concentration and focus, allowing us to be more present and attentive in our daily activities.

- **Emotional Regulation**: By observing our breath, we develop the ability to observe and detach from our thoughts and emotions, leading to greater emotional balance and resilience.

- **Enhanced Mind-Body Connection**: Breath awareness meditation deepens the connection between the mind and body, promoting overall physical and mental well-being.

Body Scan Meditation

Body scan meditation involves bringing attention to different parts of the body, observing physical sensations and releasing tension. This technique promotes relaxation, mindfulness, and self-awareness.

The benefits of body scan meditation include:

- **Stress Reduction**: Body scan meditation helps to release physical tension and promotes deep relaxation, reducing stress and anxiety.

- **Enhanced Mindfulness**: By systematically scanning the body, we develop a heightened sense of present-moment awareness and mindfulness.

- **Improved Body Awareness**: Regular practice of body scan meditation enhances body awareness, allowing us to better understand and respond to the needs of our physical body.

- **Pain Management**: Body scan meditation can be particularly beneficial for individuals dealing with chronic pain, as it helps to cultivate a non-judgmental and accepting attitude toward physical sensations.

These are just a few examples of the many meditation techniques available. It is important to remember that there is no one-size-fits-all approach to meditation. Each technique offers unique benefits, and it is up to you to explore and find the practice that resonates with you.

Whether you choose mindfulness meditation, loving-kindness meditation, or any other technique, regular practice and patience will allow you to experience the transformative power of meditation in your life.

Incorporating Mindfulness Into Everyday Activities

Mindfulness is the practice of being fully present and engaged in the present moment, without judgment. While formal meditation is a valuable way to cultivate mindfulness, it is equally important to bring this quality of awareness into our everyday activities.

By incorporating mindfulness into our daily lives, we can experience greater clarity, peace, and fulfillment. Here are some useful ways you can do just that.

Mindful Eating

Eating is a perfect opportunity to practice mindfulness. Instead of rushing through meals or eating on autopilot, try the following:

- **Savor the flavors**: Take the time to fully taste and appreciate each bite. Notice the textures, aromas, and flavors of the food. Engage all your senses in the experience.

- **Eat slowly**: Chew your food thoroughly and take your time with each bite. Pay attention to the process of eating and the sensations in your body.

- **Be present**: Avoid distractions such as screens or reading material. Instead, focus your attention on the act of eating and the nourishment it provides.

Mindful Walking

Walking is an activity that we often do without much awareness. However, by bringing mindfulness to our steps, we can transform it into a meditative practice. Here's how:

- **Slow down**: Walk at a relaxed pace, allowing yourself to fully experience each step. Be aware of the sensations in your feet and legs as they make contact with the ground.

- **Observe your surroundings**: Notice the sights, sounds, and smells around you as you walk. Engage with the environment and appreciate the beauty of nature or the urban landscape.

- **Stay present**: Whenever your mind wanders, gently bring your attention back to the physical sensations of walking. Be fully present in each moment.

Mindful Communication

Communication is an essential part of our daily lives, and practicing mindfulness in our interactions can greatly enhance the quality of our relationships. Here are some tips for mindful communication:

- **Listen attentively**: When someone is speaking, give them your full attention. Avoid interrupting or formulating responses in your mind. Instead, truly listen and be present with the speaker.

- **Speak consciously**: Before speaking, take a moment to pause and reflect. Consider the impact of your words and choose them mindfully. Speak with kindness, clarity, and intention.

- **Observe your emotions**: Notice any emotional reactions that arise during conversations. Instead of reacting impulsively, take a breath and respond with mindfulness and compassion.

Mindful Work

Many of us spend a significant portion of our day engaged in work-related activities. By bringing mindfulness to our work, we can enhance productivity, reduce stress, and find greater fulfillment. Here's how:

- **Set intentions**: Before starting your work, set clear intentions for what you hope to accomplish. This helps to bring focus and purpose to your tasks.

- **Single-task**: Instead of multitasking, focus on one task at a time. Give it your full attention and immerse yourself in the present moment.

- **Take mindful breaks**: Throughout the day, take short breaks to pause, breathe, and reset. Use these moments to bring awareness to your body and mind, releasing any tension or stress.

- **Cultivate gratitude**: Regularly remind yourself of the value and meaning behind your work. Express gratitude for the opportunities and challenges it presents.

Mindful Self-Care

Self-care is essential for our overall well-being, and practicing mindfulness can enhance the effectiveness of our self-care routines.

Here are some ways to incorporate mindfulness into self-care activities:

- **Mindful bathing:** Pay attention to the sensations of water on your skin, the scent of soap, and the feeling of relaxation. Engage your senses and be fully present in the experience.

- **Mindful breathing:** Take a few moments throughout the day to focus on your breath. Close your eyes, take deep breaths, and allow yourself to fully relax and let go of any tension.

- **Mindful movement:** Engage in activities such as yoga, stretching, or tai chi with mindfulness. Pay attention to the sensations in your body and the flow of movement.

- **Mindful rest:** When resting or engaging in leisure activities, be fully present and enjoy the experience. Avoid distractions and immerse yourself in the present moment.

Incorporating mindfulness into everyday activities requires intention and practice. Start by choosing one activity to focus on each day and gradually expand to other areas of your life. Remember to approach each moment with curiosity, non-judgment, and kindness.

With time and consistent practice, mindfulness will become a natural part of your daily routine, leading to greater presence, peace, and fulfillment.

Chapter 5

Karma and Rebirth

Karma is a fundamental concept in various spiritual and philosophical traditions, including Hinduism, Buddhism, and Jainism. It is a Sanskrit word that translates to "action" or "deed." Karma refers to the law of cause and effect, suggesting that our actions have consequences that shape our present and future experiences.

The Law of Cause and Effect

At its core, karma is based on the principle of cause and effect. It suggests that every action we perform, whether physical, verbal, or mental, creates an energetic imprint that influences our present and future experiences. Just as a seed planted in fertile soil grows into a tree, our actions plant seeds that eventually bear fruit.

According to the law of karma, positive actions lead to positive outcomes, while negative actions lead to negative outcomes. This does not necessarily mean that every action will have an immediate and direct consequence. Instead, karma operates over time, with the effects of our actions ripening when the conditions are right.

Understanding the Three Types of Karma

Karma can be categorized into three types based on the intention behind our actions:

- **Sanchita Karma**: This refers to the accumulated karma from past actions that have not yet manifested. It is the sum total of all our actions from previous lifetimes and the present one. Sanchita karma influences our current circumstances and the opportunities and challenges we encounter.

- **Prarabdha Karma**: Prarabdha karma is the portion of sanchita karma that has ripened and is currently being experienced in this lifetime. It determines the specific circumstances, relationships, and events we encounter. Prarabdha karma is like a predetermined destiny that we must live through, but we have the power to respond to it with awareness and understanding.

- **Agami Karma**: Agami karma refers to the karma that we create in the present moment through our current actions. It is the karma that will shape our future experiences. By practicing mindfulness and making conscious choices, we can influence the quality of our agami karma and create a positive path for ourselves.

The Role of Karma in Shaping Our Lives

Karma plays a significant role in shaping our lives in several ways:

- **Personal Responsibility**: The concept of karma emphasizes personal responsibility for our actions. It reminds us that we are the architects of our own destiny and that our choices have consequences. By taking responsibility for our actions, we feel empowered and can actively shape our lives.

- **Ethical Conduct**: Karma encourages ethical conduct by highlighting the importance of performing actions that are beneficial, compassionate, and aligned with moral principles. By acting with integrity and kindness, we create positive karma that leads to harmonious relationships and a sense of well-being.

- **Understanding Cause and Effect**: Karma helps us understand the relationship between our actions and their consequences. It reminds us that our present circumstances are not random but are influenced by our past actions. By reflecting on the outcomes of our actions, we can gain insight into the patterns and tendencies that shape our lives.

- **Opportunity for Growth**: Karma provides an opportunity for growth and transformation. It tells us that we can learn from our past actions and make conscious choices in the present moment to create a more positive future.

- **Interconnectedness**: Karma highlights the interconnectedness of all things. It suggests that our actions not only affect ourselves but also impact others and the world around us. By cultivating positive karma, we contribute to the well-being of others and create a ripple effect of positivity.

Working With Karma

Now we understand how karma works, it's important to know how to work with it effectively to help improve the quality of our lives and those around us. Working with karma involves cultivating awareness, mindfulness, and ethical conduct.

Here are some practices that can help us navigate the world of karma:

- **Mindful Reflection**: Regularly reflect on your actions, intentions, and the consequences they may have. Focus on self-awareness and observe the patterns and tendencies that shape your life.

- **Intentional Action**: Make a conscious effort to align your actions with positive intentions and ethical principles. Act with kindness, compassion, and integrity, knowing that your actions have the power to shape your future experiences.

- **Acceptance and Responsibility**: Accept the consequences of your past actions and take responsibility for your present circumstances. Instead of blaming external factors, focus on how you can respond to your current situation with wisdom and compassion.

- **Cultivate Virtuous Qualities**: Develop qualities such as generosity, patience, forgiveness, and gratitude. These virtues create positive karma and contribute to your own well-being and the well-being of others.

- **Practice Meditation**: Meditation helps develop mindfulness and self-awareness, allowing you to observe your thoughts, emotions, and actions with clarity. Through meditation, you can develop a deeper understanding of the nature of karma and its role in your life.

It is important to approach the concept of karma with an open mind and a sense of curiosity. While karma suggests that our actions have consequences, it does not imply that our lives are pre-determined. We can make choices and respond to our circumstances with awareness and wisdom.

Exploring Rebirth and Its Implications

The belief in rebirth is rooted in the idea that life is not limited to a single existence but is part of an ongoing process of spiritual evolution. According to this belief, the specific circumstances and experiences of each lifetime are influenced by the actions and choices made in previous lives. The cycle of rebirth continues until we achieve liberation or enlightenment, breaking free from the cycle of birth and death.

- **Ethical Responsibility**: The belief in rebirth emphasizes the ethical responsibilities of all of us. It suggests that our actions in this life have consequences that extend beyond our current existence. The choices we make and the actions we perform can shape our future lives and impact the lives of others. This understanding encourages us to act with kindness, compassion, and integrity, knowing that our actions have long-term implications.

- **Sense of Purpose**: The concept of rebirth provides a sense of purpose and meaning to life. It suggests that each lifetime offers an opportunity for growth, learning, and spiritual development. The challenges and experiences we encounter are seen as opportunities for personal evolution and the refinement of our character. This can inspire us to face life's difficulties with resilience.

- **Karma and Moral Accountability**: This belief is closely tied to the concept of karma. It suggests that our actions in this life and previous lives create an energetic imprint that influences our future experiences. Positive actions lead to positive outcomes, while negative actions lead to negative outcomes. This understanding fosters a sense of moral accountability, as we are aware that our actions have consequences that go far beyond where we are now.

- **Interconnectedness**: The belief in rebirth highlights the interconnectedness of all beings. It suggests that we are not isolated individuals but part of a larger web of existence. The actions we perform not only affect ourselves but also impact others and the world around us. This idea pushes us to cultivate compassion, empathy, and a sense of responsibility toward others.

- **Continuity of Consciousness**: This belief also implies the continuity of consciousness beyond death. It suggests that the essence of who we are, our consciousness or soul, continues to exist and evolve through multiple lifetimes. This challenges the notion of a fixed and separate self, inviting us to explore the nature of our own consciousness and the interconnectedness of all beings.

- **Opportunity for Growth and Liberation**: It offers the possibility of growth, learning, and liberation. It suggests that each lifetime provides an opportunity to overcome ignorance, attachments, and suffering, ultimately leading to enlightenment or liberation from the cycle of rebirth. We can then engage in spiritual practices, cultivate wisdom, and seek self-realization.

It is important to remember that rebirth is not a universally accepted idea and varies across different cultures and religions. While some embrace this belief as a fundamental aspect of their worldview, others may hold different beliefs about the nature of existence and the afterlife. Accepting those beliefs as just as valid as our own is vital to peace and harmony.

The belief in rebirth has implications for how we understand the purpose of life, the consequences of our actions, and our interconnectedness with others. Whether you embrace this belief or not, exploring the concept of rebirth can invite deeper reflection on the nature of existence and the potential for personal and spiritual growth.

How to Cultivate Positive Karma and Break Free from Negative Patterns

The concept of karma suggests that our actions have consequences that shape our present and future experiences. By cultivating positive karma, we can create a more harmonious and fulfilling life. Additionally, breaking free from negative patterns allows us to overcome obstacles and cultivate personal growth.

Let's explore practical ways to develop positive karma and break free from negative patterns, starting with encouraging positive karma into our lives.

- **Act with Kindness and Compassion**: Practice acts of kindness and compassion towards others. Engage in selfless acts of service, offer support to those in need, and cultivate empathy. By treating others with kindness and compassion, we create positive ripples of energy that contribute to our own well-being and the well-being of others.

- **Practice Generosity**: Cultivate a spirit of generosity by sharing your time, resources, and skills with others. Give without expecting anything in return and offer help to those who are less fortunate. Generosity not only benefits others but also brings a sense of joy and fulfillment to our own lives.

- **Speak Words of Truth and Kindness**: Practice mindful speech by speaking words that are truthful, kind, and beneficial. Avoid gossip, harsh language, and divisive speech. Instead, communicate with honesty, empathy, and respect. By using our words wisely, we create positive connections and foster harmonious relationships.

- **Cultivate Mindfulness**: Develop a regular mindfulness practice to cultivate awareness and presence in your daily life. By being fully present in each moment, you can make conscious choices and respond skillfully to situations. Mindfulness helps to reduce reactivity and allows for greater clarity and discernment in decision-making.

- **Practice Forgiveness**: Let go of grudges and practice forgiveness toward yourself and others. Holding onto resentment and anger only perpetuates negative patterns. By forgiving, we free ourselves from the burden of negative emotions and create space for healing and growth.

- **Encourage Virtuous Qualities**: Develop qualities such as patience, gratitude, humility, and honesty. These virtues contribute to positive karma and support personal growth. Regularly reflect on these qualities and make a conscious effort to embody them in your thoughts, words, and actions.

Breaking Free from Negative Patterns

- **Self-Reflection**: Engage in self-reflection to identify negative patterns and behaviors that you wish to change. Take time to understand the underlying causes and triggers for these patterns. This self-awareness is the first step towards breaking free from negative patterns.

- **Set Clear Intentions**: Set clear intentions to break free from negative patterns and cultivate positive change. Write down your intentions and remind yourself of them regularly. This clarity of purpose will help guide your actions and keep you focused on your goals.

- **Seek Support**: Reach out to supportive friends, family members, or mentors who can provide guidance and encouragement. Surround yourself with individuals who inspire and uplift you. Their support can help you stay motivated and accountable on your journey.

- **Practice Mindfulness**: Develop mindfulness to observe your thoughts, emotions, and behaviors without judgment. Notice when negative patterns arise and consciously choose to respond differently. By bringing awareness to these patterns, you can interrupt them and create space for new, positive behaviors.

- **Replace Negative Habits with Positive Ones**: Identify alternative, positive behaviors that can replace negative patterns. For example, if you tend to procrastinate, create a habit of setting small, achievable goals and rewarding yourself for completing them. By consciously replacing negative habits with positive ones, you can rewire your brain and create new, healthier patterns.

- **Practice Self-Compassion**: Be kind and compassionate toward yourself as you work to break free from negative patterns. Recognize that change takes time and effort, and treat yourself with patience, understanding, and forgiveness. Remember to celebrate small victories along the way and acknowledge your progress.

Breaking free from negative patterns and cultivating positive karma is a continuous process. It requires consistent effort, self-reflection, and self-compassion. Be patient with yourself and embrace the journey of personal growth and transformation.

Chapter 6

The Three Marks of Existence

The impermanence, suffering, and non-self nature of existence are fundamental concepts in various spiritual and philosophical traditions, including Buddhism. These concepts provide insights into the nature of reality and offer guidance on how to navigate life's ups and downs. In this chapter, let's explore these concepts and their implications for our understanding of existence.

Impermanence (Anicca)

Impermanence refers to the transient and ever-changing nature of all things. It suggests that nothing in the world, whether material or mental, remains fixed or permanent. Everything arises, exists for a period of time, and eventually ceases to exist. This includes our thoughts, emotions, relationships, and even our physical bodies.

Understanding impermanence can have profound implications for our lives. It reminds us to appreciate and cherish the present moment, as it is constantly changing. It encourages us to let go of attachments and expectations, as clinging to things that are impermanent leads to suffering. By embracing impermanence, we can cultivate a sense of freedom, adaptability, and acceptance.

When we deeply understand impermanence, we can approach life with a sense of awe and wonder. We can appreciate the beauty and preciousness of each moment, knowing that it will never be exactly the same again. This understanding can inspire us to live more fully, to cherish our relationships, and to engage in activities that bring us joy and fulfillment.

Suffering (Dukkha)

Suffering, or dukkha, is an inherent part of the human experience. It encompasses not only physical pain but also mental and emotional dissatisfaction, stress, and the unsatisfactory nature of existence. According to Buddhism, suffering arises from our attachments, desires, and the illusion of a separate self.

Recognizing the existence of suffering is the first noble truth in Buddhism. It invites us to investigate the causes and conditions that give rise to suffering in our lives. By understanding the root causes of suffering, we can work toward ending it and achieving liberation and enlightenment.

The understanding of suffering can lead to a shift in our perspective and approach to life. It encourages us to cultivate compassion and empathy toward ourselves and others. It reminds us that everyone experiences suffering in their own way and that our actions can either alleviate or contribute to the suffering of others.

Non-Self (Anatta)

The concept of non-self, or anatta, challenges the notion of a fixed and independent self. It suggests that there is no permanent, unchanging entity or soul that can be identified as "me" or "mine." Instead, our experience is a constantly changing and interconnected process of physical and mental experiences.

The understanding of non-self has profound implications for our sense of identity and attachment. It invites us to question the illusion of a separate and permanent self and to recognize the interdependence of all beings. By letting go of the attachment to a fixed identity, we can cultivate compassion, empathy, and a deeper understanding of the interconnected nature of existence.

The concept of non-self can liberate us from the suffering that arises from clinging to a fixed identity. It allows us to let go of the ego-driven desires and attachments that cause us pain and dissatisfaction. This all leads to a more compassionate and harmonious way of living.

Implications for Existence

Exploring the impermanence, suffering, and non-self nature of existence can lead to a shift in our perspective and approach to life. Here are some of the most common effects of realizing and understanding these concepts:

- **Embracing Change**: Recognizing impermanence encourages us to embrace change and let go of attachments. It reminds us that everything is in a constant state of flux and that clinging to things that are impermanent leads to suffering. By embracing change, we can find greater peace and adaptability in the face of life's challenges.

- **Fostering Calmness**: Understanding the nature of suffering invites us to cultivate calmness, a balanced and accepting attitude toward both pleasure and pain. By recognizing the unsatisfactory nature of existence, we can develop resilience and a deeper appreciation for the moments of joy and contentment that arise amidst the inevitable challenges of life.

- **Practicing Non-Attachment**: The concept of non-self challenges our attachments and identification with a fixed identity. By letting go of the illusion of a separate self, we can develop a sense of non-attachment and reduce the suffering that arises from clinging and grasping. This practice allows for greater freedom, flexibility, and openness to the ever-changing nature of existence.

- **Increased Compassion**: Recognizing the interconnected nature of existence encourages us to offer compassion and empathy toward all beings. By understanding that we are not separate from others, we can develop a sense of responsibility and care for the well-being of all. This understanding fosters a more compassionate and harmonious way of living.

- **Seeking Liberation**: Understanding these concepts provides a framework for seeking liberation or enlightenment. By investigating the causes of suffering and developing wisdom and compassion, we can work toward the end of suffering and the realization of our true nature.

Finding Peace and Liberation Through Acceptance

The acceptance of impermanence, suffering, and non-self is a transformative journey that can lead to personal growth and spiritual awakening. Let's explore how acceptance of these truths can lead to peace and liberation.

- **Embracing Impermanence**: Accepting the impermanence of all things allows us to let go of attachments and expectations. Instead of resisting change, we learn to flow with the natural rhythms of life. This acceptance brings a sense of peace and freedom, as we no longer cling to things that are inherently transient.

- **Transforming Suffering**: Accepting the reality of suffering is the first step toward transforming it. When we acknowledge and accept our own suffering, we can approach it with compassion and understanding. Instead of resisting or avoiding pain, we learn to be present with it, allowing it to teach us valuable lessons. This acceptance of suffering opens the door to healing and growth, leading to greater resilience and inner strength.

- **Letting Go of the Illusion of Self**: Accepting the non-self nature of existence liberates us from the burden of a fixed and separate identity. By recognizing that there is no permanent, unchanging self, we can let go of ego-driven desires and attachments. This acceptance allows us to experience a sense of interconnectedness and interdependence with all beings. We no longer need to defend or protect a limited sense of self, and instead, we can cultivate a deep sense of peace and unity.

- **Transcending the Cycle of Suffering**: Through acceptance of impermanence, suffering, and non-self, we can transcend the cycle of suffering. By understanding the causes and conditions that give rise to suffering, we can work toward ending it. Through this process, we can attain liberation or enlightenment, experiencing a profound sense of peace, freedom, and liberation from suffering.

Of course, this whole journey requires self-reflection, mindfulness, and a commitment to personal growth. Through acceptance, we can find deep meaning and fulfillment in the ever-changing nature of existence.

CHAPTER 7

Buddhist Ethics and Morality

Buddhism encompasses a wide range of ethical guidelines and principles. We've explored some of these, but let's group them all together and delve deeper to understand exactly how these principles can guide us toward leading a moral and compassionate life.

The Five Precepts

The Five Precepts are the basic moral guidelines that Buddhists strive to follow. They are:

- **Refraining from taking life:** This precept encourages Buddhists to avoid causing harm to any living being. It promotes the value of non-violence and respect for all forms of life. This principle extends beyond humans to include animals and even insects. Buddhists believe that all beings have the potential for enlightenment and should be treated with kindness and compassion.

- **Refraining from taking what is not given:** Buddhists are encouraged to practice honesty and refrain from stealing or taking what does not belong to them. This precept emphasizes the importance of respecting the property and possessions of others. It promotes the idea of contentment and discourages greed and materialism.

- **Refraining from sexual misconduct:** This precept promotes ethical and responsible behavior in relationships. It emphasizes the importance of mutual consent, respect, and fidelity.

Buddhists are encouraged to cultivate loving and compassionate relationships that are based on trust and understanding.

- **Refraining from false speech:** Buddhists are encouraged to speak truthfully and avoid lying, gossiping, or using harsh or hurtful words. This precept highlights the power of speech and its impact on others. It promotes the value of honesty, integrity, and mindful communication.

- **Refraining from intoxicants:** This precept advises against the consumption of substances that cloud the mind and lead to negative behaviors. It encourages us to cultivate clarity and mindfulness in our actions and decisions. By avoiding intoxicants, Buddhists aim to maintain a clear and focused mind, which is essential for spiritual growth and ethical conduct.

The Eightfold Path

We've explored the Eightfold Path in a previous chapter, and we know it is a fundamental teaching in Buddhism that provides a comprehensive framework for ethical conduct. It consists of eight interconnected aspects that guide individuals towards liberation from suffering, including:

- Right Understanding
- Right Intention
- Right Speech
- Right Action
- Right Livelihood
- Right Effort
- Right Mindfulness
- Right Concentration

Compassion and Loving-Kindness

Buddhism places a strong emphasis on showing compassion and loving-kindness toward all beings. Practicing compassion involves developing empathy, understanding, and a genuine concern for the well-being of others. Buddhists are encouraged to extend their compassion beyond their immediate circle and embrace all living beings. This principle promotes acts of kindness, generosity, and selflessness.

Compassion and loving-kindness are not limited to humans but extend to animals and the environment as well. Buddhists recognize the interconnectedness of all life and strive to alleviate suffering wherever it is found. By fostering compassion, we develop a deep sense of empathy and contribute to a more harmonious and compassionate world.

Non-violence

Buddhism promotes non-violence as a core principle. Buddhists are encouraged to resolve conflicts peacefully and to avoid causing harm to any living being, including animals. This principle extends to all aspects of life, including thoughts, words, and actions.

Buddhists believe that violence only perpetuates suffering and hinders spiritual growth. By practicing non-violence, individuals contribute to a more peaceful and compassionate society.

Mindfulness

Mindfulness is a central practice in Buddhism that involves being fully present and aware of our thoughts, feelings, and actions. By focusing on mindfulness, we can develop a greater sense of self-awareness and make conscious choices that align with ethical principles.

Mindfulness helps us to act with intention and integrity, avoiding impulsive or harmful behavior.

Mindfulness also extends to the way Buddhists interact with the world around them. It encourages individuals to be mindful of their impact on others and the environment. By practicing mindfulness, we develop a deep sense of responsibility and become more attuned to the ethical implications of our actions.

These are just a few of the major ethical guidelines and principles in Buddhism. They provide a moral compass for Buddhists, guiding them toward leading a life of compassion, mindfulness, and non-harm.

Understanding the Importance of Compassion, Kindness, and Non-Harming

Compassion, kindness, and non-harming are fundamental values that hold great significance in Buddhism as well as other belief systems. Understanding their importance can have a great impact on our personal well-being, relationships, and the overall harmony of society.

Let's delve deeper into each of these principles:

Compassion

Compassion is the ability to empathize with the suffering of others and the desire to alleviate it. It involves recognizing the interconnectedness of all beings and responding with kindness and understanding. Compassion goes beyond sympathy or pity; it is an active response that seeks to alleviate suffering and promote the well-being of others.

Practicing compassion allows us to cultivate a sense of connection and empathy toward others. It helps us develop a deeper understanding of their struggles and challenges. By extending compassion, we create a supportive and caring environment where individuals feel seen, heard, and valued. Compassion also fosters forgiveness and reconciliation, allowing us to let go of resentment and promote healing.

Kindness

Kindness means being friendly, generous, and considerate toward others. It involves acts of goodwill, warmth, and genuine care. Kindness can be expressed through simple gestures, such as a smile, a kind word, or a helping hand. It is a powerful force that has the ability to uplift spirits, create positive connections, and create a sense of belonging.

Practicing kindness not only benefits others but also enhances our own well-being. When we engage in acts of kindness, our brains release oxytocin, a hormone associated with feelings of happiness and well-being. Kindness also promotes a positive ripple effect, inspiring others to also act with kindness, thereby creating a more compassionate and harmonious society.

Non-harming

Non-harming, also known as non-violence or ahimsa, is the principle of refraining from causing harm to ourselves, others, and the environment. It involves fostering a deep respect for all forms of life and recognizing the interconnectedness of our actions. Non-harming extends beyond physical violence and includes refraining from harmful speech, thoughts, and intentions.

Practicing non-harming requires us to cultivate mindfulness and awareness of the impact of our actions. It encourages us to find peaceful resolutions to conflicts, to treat others with respect and dignity, and to live in harmony with nature. Non-harming promotes a culture of peace, justice, and sustainability, fostering a world where all beings can thrive.

These principles remind us of our shared humanity and the responsibility we have toward one another and the planet. By embodying these values in our daily lives, we contribute to the well-being of ourselves, others, and the world around us.

Compassion, kindness, and non-harming are not only moral principles but also powerful catalysts for personal growth and societal transformation. They remind us of the inherent goodness within each individual and the potential for positive change.

Applying Buddhist Ethics in Personal and Social Contexts

Applying Buddhist ethics in personal and social contexts can have a transformative impact on us and society as a whole. Buddhist ethics provide a framework for cultivating wisdom, compassion, and mindfulness in our daily lives.

Let's explore how these principles can be applied in personal and social contexts:

Personal Context

- **Self-reflection:** Buddhist ethics encourage us to engage in self-reflection and introspection. By examining our thoughts, emotions, and actions, we can gain insight into our own patterns and tendencies. This self-awareness allows us to identify areas where we may be causing harm or acting unskillfully and provides an opportunity for personal growth and transformation.

- **Mindfulness:** We've already explored that mindfulness is a central practice in Buddhism. By focusing on mindfulness, we can observe our thoughts and emotions without judgment, and make conscious choices that align with ethical principles. Mindfulness helps us develop greater clarity, discernment, and intentionality in our personal lives.

- **Practicing the Five Precepts:** The Five Precepts, which include refraining from harming, stealing, engaging in sexual misconduct, lying, and consuming intoxicants, provide a moral compass for personal conduct. By consciously practicing these precepts, we can ensure our behavior is ethical and create a foundation of integrity and compassion in our lives.

Social Context:

- **Compassionate Action:** Buddhism emphasizes the importance of compassionate action toward others. This involves extending kindness, empathy, and support to those in need. By actively engaging in acts of service and generosity, we contribute to the well-being of others and develop a sense of interconnectedness and community.

- **Non-Violent Communication:** Buddhism encourages us to practice non-violent communication, which involves speaking truthfully, kindly, and with empathy. Compassionate and mindful communication helps us foster understanding, resolve conflicts peacefully, and build harmonious relationships.

- **Social Justice and Equality:** Buddhist ethics call for the recognition of the inherent dignity and worth of all beings. This includes advocating for social justice, equality, and the alleviation of suffering. By actively working toward creating a more just and equitable society, we contribute to the well-being and happiness of all individuals.

- **Environmental Stewardship:** Buddhism emphasizes the interconnectedness of all life and the importance of living in harmony with nature. Applying Buddhist ethics in a social context involves practicing environmental stewardship and promoting sustainable living. By cultivating mindfulness of our impact on the environment and taking steps to reduce harm, we contribute to the preservation of the planet for future generations.

Applying Buddhist ethics in personal and social contexts requires a commitment to self-awareness, compassion, and mindful action.

It involves integrating ethical principles into our daily lives and actively working toward creating a more compassionate and harmonious world.

By embodying these principles, we not only benefit ourselves but also inspire and uplift those around us.

Chapter 8

The Three Jewels of Buddhism

Taking refuge in the Buddha, Dharma, and Sangha is a significant aspect of Buddhist practice. It represents a deep commitment to the teachings and principles of Buddhism and serves as a foundation for spiritual growth and liberation.

We know that the Buddha, Siddhartha Gautama, is the historical figure who attained enlightenment and became awakened. Taking refuge in the Buddha means acknowledging and seeking inspiration from his teachings, wisdom, and example. The Buddha serves as a guide and a source of inspiration for those on the path to liberation. By taking refuge in the Buddha, we express our trust in his teachings and his ability to show the way to freedom from suffering.

It also involves studying his teachings, contemplating their meaning, and applying them in our daily lives. The Buddha represents the potential for awakening that exists within each individual, reminding us that liberation is attainable through diligent practice and self-transformation.

The Dharma

The Dharma refers to the teachings of the Buddha, the universal truth that he discovered and shared with the world. Taking refuge in the Dharma means recognizing the truth and validity of these teachings and relying on them as a guide for personal transformation.

The Dharma encompasses the Four Noble Truths, the Eightfold Path, and various other teachings that provide a comprehensive framework for understanding and navigating the human condition. It offers profound insights into the nature of suffering, the impermanence of all phenomena, and the interdependent nature of reality. Additionally, it provides practical instructions on how to cultivate ethical conduct, develop mindfulness, and cultivate wisdom.

By taking refuge in the Dharma, we commit to studying, practicing, and embodying these teachings in our daily lives. The Dharma serves as a compass, guiding us toward liberation and the realization of our true nature.

The Sangha

The Sangha refers to a community of people who support and inspire each other on the path to awakening. Taking refuge in the Sangha means seeking refuge in the spiritual community, finding support, guidance, and inspiration from fellow Buddhists. The Sangha provides a supportive environment where individuals can learn, practice, and grow together.

The Sangha consists of monastic communities as well as lay practitioners. Monastic communities, such as monks and nuns, dedicate their lives to the practice and preservation of the Dharma. They serve as a source of inspiration and guidance, which can be integrated into our everyday lives, balancing spiritual practice with our everyday responsibilities.

By taking refuge in the Sangha, we commit to actively participating in and contributing to the spiritual community. The Sangha serves as a reminder that the path to awakening is not a solitary endeavor but one that is supported by a community of like-minded people.

Taking refuge in the Buddha, Dharma, and Sangha is a significant aspect of Buddhist practice. It represents a deep commitment to the teachings, principles, and community of Buddhism. By taking refuge, we express our trust in the Buddha's teachings, rely on the Dharma as a guide, and seek support and inspiration from the Sangha.

Taking refuge serves as a foundation for personal growth, spiritual development, and the development of wisdom, compassion, and mindfulness. It is a reminder that the path to awakening is not a solitary journey but one that is supported by the wisdom of the Buddha, the truth of the Dharma, and a community of fellow Buddhists.

Understanding the Role of Each Jewel in Our Spiritual Journey

In Buddhism, the Three Jewels, also known as the Triple Gem, play a crucial role in our spiritual journey. Each jewel represents a distinct aspect that supports and guides us on the path to liberation.

Let's explore the role of each jewel in more detail:

The Buddha

The first jewel represents the Buddha. The Buddha serves as a supreme teacher and an embodiment of wisdom and compassion. Understanding the role of the Buddha involves recognizing his unique qualities and the significance of his teachings.

The Buddha's role is multifaceted. He serves as an inspiration, demonstrating that liberation from suffering is attainable for all beings. His teachings provide guidance on how to cultivate wisdom, compassion, and mindfulness. By studying the life and teachings of the Buddha, we gain insight into the nature of existence and the path to liberation.

The Buddha also serves as a refuge, a source of inspiration and support. Taking refuge in the Buddha means placing trust in his teachings and relying on his guidance. By following the example set by the Buddha, we can develop the qualities necessary for our own awakening.

The Dharma

The second jewel represents the Dharma, which refers to the teachings of the Buddha. The Dharma encompasses the universal truths and principles that the Buddha discovered and shared with the world. Understanding the role of the Dharma involves recognizing its significance as a guide for personal transformation.

The Dharma provides a comprehensive framework for understanding the nature of suffering, the causes of suffering, and the path to liberation. It offers profound insights into the impermanence of all phenomena, the interdependent nature of reality, and the development of ethical conduct, mindfulness, and wisdom.

The role of the Dharma is to serve as a map, guiding us on our spiritual journey. By studying and contemplating the Dharma, we gain a deeper understanding of the nature of reality and the causes of suffering. The Dharma provides practical instructions on how to live a skillful and meaningful life, leading to liberation from suffering.

The Sangha

The third jewel represents the Sangha, which refers to the community of Buddhists who support and inspire each other on the path to awakening. The Sangha plays a vital role in providing guidance, support, and a sense of belonging.

Monastic communities, such as monks and nuns, dedicate their lives to the practice and preservation of the Dharma.

The Three Jewels provide a foundation for personal growth, spiritual development, and the cultivation of wisdom, compassion, and mindfulness. They serve as a reminder that the path to awakening is not only about personal transformation but also about contributing to the well-being and liberation of all beings.

Finding Support and Guidance Within the Buddhist Community

Finding support and guidance within the Buddhist community can be a deeply enriching and transformative aspect of a spiritual journey.

Let's explore in more detail how the Buddhist community offers support and guidance, and the various ways we can benefit from being part of it:

- **Shared Understanding and Connection:** Within the Buddhist community, people share a common understanding of the teachings and principles of Buddhism. This shared understanding creates a sense of belonging and connection. Being part of a community of like-minded individuals who are on a similar path can be comforting and inspiring. It provides a space where we can openly discuss our experiences, challenges, and insights, knowing that they will be met with understanding and support. This sense of connection fosters a feeling of unity and encourages us to continue our spiritual journey with renewed enthusiasm.

- **Spiritual Friendship and Support:** The Buddhist community offers the opportunity to develop spiritual friendships, also known as kalyana-mittata. These friendships are based on shared values, mutual support, and a commitment to spiritual growth. Spiritual friends provide encouragement, guidance, and accountability on the path to awakening. They can offer insights, share their own experiences, and provide a listening ear during times of difficulty. Spiritual friendships within the Buddhist community can be a source of inspiration and motivation, as we can learn from one another and support each other's progress.

- **Guidance from Experienced Buddhists:** The Buddhist community often includes experienced individuals, such as monastics or long-time practitioners, who can offer guidance and mentorship. These people have dedicated their lives to the practice and study of Buddhism, and their wisdom and experience can be invaluable for those seeking guidance. They can provide teachings, answer questions, and offer practical advice on integrating the teachings into daily life. Their presence and guidance can help us navigate challenges and deepen our understanding of the teachings.

- **Communal Practice and Collective Energy:** The Buddhist community provides opportunities for communal practice, such as group meditation sessions, retreats, and ceremonies. Engaging in communal practice can be a powerful experience, as the collective energy of the group supports and enhances individual practice. Meditating together, chanting, or engaging in other forms of practice as a community can deepen our own practice and create a sense of unity and connection. Communal practice also offers the chance to learn from others and observe different approaches to the path. The collective energy generated during communal practice can be uplifting and transformative, fostering a sense of shared purpose and strengthening the spiritual bond within the community.

- **Service and Volunteering:** The Buddhist community often engages in acts of service and volunteering, which can be a meaningful way to contribute and find support. Engaging in service projects, such as helping the less fortunate or participating in environmental initiatives, allows us to embody the teachings of compassion and generosity. It also provides an opportunity to connect with others who share similar values and aspirations. Serving the community can be a source of inspiration and a way to deepen our understanding of the teachings through practical application. Engaging in service and volunteering within the Buddhist community fosters a sense of interconnectedness and encourages us to live in alignment with the principles of Buddhism.

Finding support and guidance within the Buddhist community is not only beneficial for individuals but also contributes to the overall well-being and growth of the community itself. By actively participating in the community, we create a network of support and contribute to the collective wisdom and compassion of the Sangha.

The Buddhist community serves as a refuge, a place where we can find solace, inspiration, and guidance on our spiritual journey. It provides a nurturing environment that encourages personal growth, fosters deep connections, and cultivates the qualities of wisdom, compassion, and mindfulness.

CHAPTER 9

Buddhist Cosmology and Symbolism

Buddhism encompasses many cosmological beliefs and a great deal of symbolism that provides a framework for understanding the nature of existence and the path to liberation. These beliefs and symbols offer insights into the interconnectedness of all phenomena and the ultimate goal of attaining enlightenment.

Interconnectedness and Dependent Origination

At the core of Buddhist cosmology is the concept of interconnectedness and dependent origination. Buddhists believe that all phenomena are interdependent and arise in dependence on various causes and conditions. This understanding extends to all aspects of existence, from the physical world to the realm of thoughts and emotions.

The belief in dependent origination emphasizes the impermanence and interconnected nature of reality, highlighting the importance of understanding the causes and conditions that give rise to suffering and liberation.

The Wheel of Life (Bhavachakra)

The Wheel of Life, also known as the Bhavachakra, is a powerful symbol in Buddhism that represents the cycle of existence and the process of samsara. The wheel is divided into six realms, each representing different states of existence, including the realms of gods, humans, animals, hungry ghosts, hell beings, and jealous gods.

The Wheel of Life serves as a visual reminder of the impermanence and unsatisfactory nature of cyclic existence, and the importance of breaking free from this cycle through spiritual practice.

Mandalas

Mandalas are intricate geometric patterns that serve as visual representations of the universe and the enlightened mind. Mandalas are often used as objects of meditation and are created using various symbols and colors that hold specific meanings.

Mandalas symbolize the interconnectedness of all phenomena and the potential for enlightenment within each individual. They serve as a tool for focusing the mind and cultivating a sense of harmony and balance.

Bodhisattvas

Bodhisattvas are enlightened beings who have chosen to postpone their own liberation in order to help others attain enlightenment. They are revered figures in Buddhism and serve as symbols of compassion, wisdom, and selfless service.

Bodhisattvas are depicted in various forms and are often associated with specific qualities or virtues. Their presence in Buddhist cosmology represents the ideal of selfless compassion and the aspiration to alleviate the suffering of all beings.

Pure Lands

Pure Lands, such as Amitabha Buddha's Pure Land of Sukhavati, are celestial realms believed to be inhabited by enlightened beings. Pure Lands are depicted as idyllic and blissful realms where Buddhists can be reborn after death to continue their spiritual journey toward enlightenment.

Pure Lands serve as symbols of the ultimate goal of liberation and provide inspiration and aspiration for Buddhists.

Stupas

Stupas are sacred structures that serve as symbols of enlightenment and the presence of the Buddha. They are often built to enshrine relics or sacred objects associated with the Buddha or other enlightened beings.

Stupas represent the enlightened mind and serve as reminders of the Buddha's teachings and the potential for awakening within every person. They are considered places of pilgrimage and meditation, where Buddhists can cultivate devotion and connect with the spiritual qualities they represent.

Mudras and Hand Gestures

Mudras are symbolic hand gestures used in Buddhist rituals and iconography. Each mudra holds a specific meaning and represents different aspects of the Buddha's teachings or qualities. For example, the gesture of the Buddha's hand touching the earth (Bhumisparsha mudra) symbolizes the moment of enlightenment and the Buddha's calling the earth as a witness to his awakening.

Mudras serve as visual representations of spiritual qualities and can be used in meditation to cultivate specific states of mind.

These cosmological beliefs and symbols in Buddhism provide us with a framework for understanding the nature of existence and the path to liberation. They serve as visual reminders of the interconnectedness of all phenomena, the impermanence of existence, and the potential for enlightenment within each person.

By contemplating and engaging with these symbols, we can deepen our understanding of the teachings and cultivate qualities such as compassion, wisdom, and mindfulness.

It is important to note that while these cosmological beliefs and symbols hold significance in Buddhism, they are not meant to be taken literally. They are tools for contemplation, meditation, and inspiration, guiding us on our spiritual journey. The ultimate goal of Buddhism is to transcend all concepts and symbols, realizing the true nature of reality beyond words and symbols.

Understanding the significance of sacred symbols and rituals

Sacred symbols and rituals serve as powerful tools for connecting with the divine, expressing devotion, and deepening spiritual practice. They are used in all world religions.

Let's explore the significance of sacred symbols and rituals in more detail:

Sacred Symbols

Sacred symbols are visual representations that carry deep spiritual meaning and evoke a sense of reverence and awe. They can take various forms, such as geometric patterns, images, or objects. These symbols often embody profound concepts, teachings, or archetypal energies.

Here are a few examples:

- **Cross:** The cross is a widely recognized symbol in Christianity, representing the crucifixion and resurrection of Jesus Christ. It symbolizes sacrifice, redemption, and the triumph of life over death.

- **Om:** Om is a sacred symbol in Hinduism, Buddhism, and Jainism. It represents the primordial sound of the universe and the ultimate reality. Chanting or meditating on the sound of Om is believed to connect individuals with the divine and bring about a sense of peace and unity.

- **Yin and Yang:** The Yin and Yang symbol is rooted in Chinese philosophy and represents the interplay of opposing forces in the universe. It symbolizes the balance and harmony between complementary energies, such as light and dark, masculine and feminine, and active and passive.

- **Star of David:** The Star of David is a symbol in Judaism, consisting of two interlocking triangles. It represents the connection between the divine and human realms, as well as the unity of the Jewish people.

Sacred symbols guide individuals on their spiritual journey and deepen their connection with the divine. They can evoke a sense of awe, inspire contemplation, and provide a focal point for meditation or prayer.

Rituals

Rituals are symbolic actions or ceremonies that are performed in a prescribed manner. They often involve specific gestures, words, or objects and are conducted within a sacred or ceremonial space.

Rituals serve multiple purposes, including:

- **Expressing Devotion:** Rituals provide a means for us to express our devotion and reverence toward the divine. Through rituals, we can demonstrate our commitment, gratitude, and love for the sacred. For example, lighting candles, offering incense, or reciting prayers can be acts of devotion in various religious traditions.

- **Creating Sacred Space:** Rituals help create a sacred space that is separate from ordinary life. This space is often consecrated and imbued with spiritual energy. By entering this sacred space, we can temporarily detach from the mundane world and connect with the divine. Rituals can involve purification, chanting, or the use of specific objects to sanctify the space.

- **Marking Transitions:** Rituals are often performed to mark significant life transitions, such as birth, coming of age, marriage, and death. These rituals provide a sense of continuity, meaning, and support during times of change. They help us navigate these transitions and connect with the spiritual dimensions of life.

- **Practicing Mindfulness:** Rituals can be a form of mindfulness practice, bringing us into the present moment and fostering a sense of awareness and presence. By engaging in rituals with intention and focus, we can cultivate a deeper connection with the divine and develop a heightened sense of mindfulness.

- **Strengthening Community:** Rituals often involve communal participation, bringing people together in shared spiritual experiences. They foster a sense of belonging, unity, and support within the community. Rituals can strengthen social bonds, promote cooperation, and provide a sense of collective identity.

Sacred symbols and rituals are deeply ingrained in the fabric of religious and spiritual traditions. They serve as vehicles for connecting with the divine, expressing devotion, and deepening spiritual practice.

It is important to note that the significance of sacred symbols and rituals can vary across different cultures and religious traditions. The interpretation and understanding of these symbols and rituals are shaped by the specific beliefs, teachings, and cultural contexts in which they are practiced.

It is essential to approach sacred symbols and rituals with respect, openness, and a willingness to learn from the perspectives of those who hold them dear.

How to Interpret and Engage With Buddhist Cosmology

Buddhist cosmology requires an open and contemplative approach that embraces the richness and diversity of Buddhist teachings. Buddhist cosmology encompasses many concepts, symbols, and narratives that offer insights into the nature of existence and the path to liberation.

Here are some suggestions on how to interpret and engage with Buddhist cosmology in an educational style:

- **Study the Teachings:** Begin by studying the teachings of Buddhism, including the foundational texts such as the Sutras, commentaries, and teachings of respected Buddhist teachers. Familiarize yourself with the cosmological concepts presented in these texts. Take time to read and reflect upon the teachings, considering their implications for your own life and spiritual journey.

- **Embrace Symbolic Language:** Buddhist cosmology often uses symbolic language to convey profound truths that may be challenging to express directly. Embrace the symbolic nature of the teachings and recognize that they are meant to point to deeper realities rather than being taken literally. Approach the symbols with curiosity and an open mind, allowing them to trigger contemplation and insight.

- **Seek Guidance:** Engage in discussions and seek guidance from experienced Buddhists, teachers, or scholars who have a deep understanding of Buddhist cosmology. Their insights and perspectives can provide valuable guidance and help clarify any questions or uncertainties you may have. Engaging in dialogue with others can deepen your understanding and offer different perspectives on the cosmological teachings.

- **Foster Mindfulness and Insight:** Cultivate mindfulness and insight through meditation and contemplative practices. By developing a deep awareness of your own mind and experiences, you can directly explore the teachings and their relevance to your own life. This experiential understanding can bring the cosmological concepts to life and deepen your engagement with them.

- **Focus on Practical Application:** While Buddhist cosmology may involve complex concepts and narratives, it is ultimately meant to be applied in practical ways to transform your life. Focus on how the cosmological teachings can inform and guide your daily thoughts, actions, and relationships. Consider how the teachings on interconnectedness, impermanence, and compassion can shape your worldview and influence your interactions with others.

- **Embrace the Mystery:** Buddhist cosmology encompasses vast and profound concepts that may not be fully comprehensible to you. Embrace the mystery and recognize that some aspects of the cosmology may remain beyond our intellectual grasp.

- **Connect with the Symbolism:** Engage with the symbolism present in Buddhist cosmology through visualizations, rituals, or artistic expressions. Mandalas, sacred images, or ritual practices can serve as gateways to connect with the cosmological teachings on a deeper level.

- **Integrate with Ethical Conduct:** Remember that Buddhist cosmology is not separate from ethical conduct and virtues. The teachings on interconnectedness and compassion are intimately linked with how we relate to ourselves, others, and the world. Integrate cosmological teachings into your ethical conduct, cultivating kindness, compassion, and wisdom in your interactions and actions.

In interpreting and engaging with Buddhist cosmology, it is important to approach the teachings with an open heart and mind. Recognize that different interpretations and understandings may exist, and that your own understanding may evolve over time.

Embrace the transformative potential of the cosmological teachings and allow them to guide you on your own spiritual journey toward liberation and awakening.

Chapter 10

Buddhist Scriptures and Texts

The sacred texts of Buddhism hold immense significance as they contain the teachings and wisdom of the Buddha and his disciples. These texts serve as a guide and provide insights into the nature of existence, the path to liberation, and the cultivation of wisdom and compassion.

Two prominent collections of sacred texts in Buddhism are the Tripitaka and the sutras. Let's explore these texts in more detail:

Tripitaka

The Tripitaka, also known as the "Three Baskets," is the earliest and most authoritative collection of Buddhist scriptures. It is divided into three sections or "baskets" that cover various aspects of the Buddha's teachings:

- **Vinaya Pitaka:** This section focuses on monastic discipline and rules for the Sangha (community of monks and nuns). It provides guidelines for ethical conduct, including rules for personal conduct, communal harmony, and the resolution of conflicts within the monastic community.

- **Sutta Pitaka:** The Sutta Pitaka contains the words of the Buddha, known as sutras or suttas. This covers a wide range of topics, including ethics, meditation, mindfulness, wisdom, and the nature of reality. The Sutta Pitaka is further divided into five collections, known as the Nikayas, which include the Digha Nikaya (Long Discourses), Majjhima Nikaya (Middle-

Length Discourses), Samyutta Nikaya (Connected Discourses), Anguttara Nikaya (Numerical Discourses), and Khuddaka Nikaya (Collection of Miscellaneous Texts).

- **Abhidhamma Pitaka:** The Abhidhamma Pitaka is a more analytical and philosophical section of the Tripitaka. It delves into the detailed analysis of mind, mental factors, and the nature of reality. The Abhidhamma provides a systematic framework for understanding the workings of the mind and the nature of existence.

Sutras

Sutras are individual teachings attributed to the Buddha or his close disciples. They are found in various collections and are revered as sacred texts in different Buddhist traditions. The sutras cover a wide range of topics, including ethics, meditation, wisdom, compassion, and the nature of reality.

Some well-known sutras include the Heart Sutra, Diamond Sutra, Lotus Sutra, and the Dhammapada.

The sutras often feature metaphorical language, parables, and poetic expressions to describe profound truths. They provide guidance on how to live a virtuous life, develop mindfulness and wisdom, and attain liberation from suffering. The sutras are considered to be the words of the Buddha and are highly respected and studied by Buddhist practitioners.

Studying the sacred texts of Buddhism, such as the Tripitaka and sutras, is an essential part of Buddhist practice. The texts serve as a source of inspiration, guidance, and contemplation, providing a roadmap for the spiritual journey.

As always, it's important to note that the interpretation and understanding of these texts can vary across different Buddhist traditions and schools. Scholars and practitioners conduct textual analysis, comparative studies, and contemplative practices to explore the layers of meaning within the texts. The texts are not meant to be taken literally but are to be contemplated and applied in our own lives.

Exploring the Teachings and Wisdom Contained Within Them

Exploring the teachings and wisdom contained within the sacred texts of Buddhism, such as the Tripitaka and sutras, is a transformative journey. So, what can we learn from these important texts?

- **Ethical Conduct:** The sacred texts emphasize the importance of ethical conduct as a foundation for spiritual practice. They provide guidelines for moral behavior, emphasizing virtues such as non-harming, honesty, compassion, and mindfulness. The teachings encourage us to cultivate ethical conduct in our thoughts, speech, and actions, recognizing that it is essential for personal well-being and the well-being of others.

- **Mindfulness and Meditation:** They highlight the practice of mindfulness and meditation as essential tools for developing awareness, concentration, and insight. They provide instructions on various meditation techniques, including breath awareness, loving-kindness, and insight meditation. The teachings emphasize the cultivation of present-moment awareness, the observation of mental and physical phenomena, and the development of a clear and focused mind.

- **Impermanence and Emptiness:** The texts explore the fundamental Buddhist teachings of impermanence and emptiness. They emphasize that everything is impermanent and subject to change. This encourages us to develop a deep understanding of impermanence and emptiness as a means to overcome attachment, craving, and suffering.

- **Four Noble Truths:** The Four Noble Truths form the core of the Buddha's teachings. The texts expound on these truths, which include the truth of suffering, the truth of the origin of suffering, the truth of the cessation of suffering, and the truth of the path leading to the cessation of suffering. The teachings provide a comprehensive framework for understanding the nature of suffering, its causes, and the path to liberation from suffering.

- **Compassion and Loving-Kindness:** The sacred texts emphasize the cultivation of compassion and loving-kindness as essential qualities on the spiritual path. They provide teachings on the practice of metta (loving-kindness) meditation and encourage us to extend compassion and kindness to all.

- **Wisdom and Insight:** These texts offer profound teachings on wisdom and insight, guiding us toward a deeper understanding of the nature of reality. They explore concepts such as dependent origination, the aggregates, and the Three Marks of Existence (impermanence, suffering, and non-self).

- **Liberation and Enlightenment:** They provide guidance on the path to liberation and enlightenment. They describe the qualities and characteristics of an awakened being, emphasizing the cultivation of wisdom, compassion, and ethical conduct. The teachings offer various methods and practices to overcome ignorance, craving, and attachment, leading to the ultimate goal of liberation from suffering and the realization of our true nature.

Exploring the teachings and wisdom contained within these sacred texts requires a dedicated and contemplative approach. It involves studying the texts, reflecting on their meaning, and integrating the teachings into our own lives and practice. Engaging with the teachings through contemplation, meditation, and ethical conduct allows us to deepen our understanding, transform our lives, and foster wisdom and compassion.

How to Approach and Study Buddhist Scriptures

Studying Buddhist scriptures can be a deeply enriching and transformative experience. Here are some steps to help you approach and study Buddhist scriptures in an educational and meaningful way:

- **Cultivate a Mindset of Openness and Curiosity**: Approaching Buddhist scriptures requires an open mind and a genuine curiosity to learn. Recognize that these texts contain wisdom and insights that can challenge your existing beliefs and expand your understanding of life and spirituality.

- **Start with the Basics**: Begin your study by familiarizing yourself with the foundational teachings of Buddhism. This includes understanding the Four Noble Truths, the Eightfold Path, and the concept of impermanence. These core principles provide a solid framework for comprehending the deeper teachings found in the scriptures.

- **Choose a Specific Text or Topic**: Buddhist scriptures are vast and diverse, so it's helpful to choose a specific text or topic to focus on. This could be the Dhammapada, the Sutta Pitaka, or teachings on mindfulness and meditation. By narrowing your focus, you can delve deeper into the chosen subject and gain a more comprehensive understanding.

- **Seek Guidance from Teachers or Experts:** Studying Buddhist scriptures can be complex, and having guidance from experienced teachers or experts can greatly enhance your learning. Seek out qualified teachers, attend meditation retreats, or join study groups where you can discuss and clarify your understanding of the scriptures.

- **Read and Reflect**: Read the chosen text or scripture attentively, taking your time to absorb the teachings. Reflect on the meaning and implications of the teachings in your own life.

Consider how you can apply these teachings to cultivate inner peace, compassion, and wisdom.

- **Practice Mindfulness and Meditation**: Buddhist scriptures often emphasize the importance of mindfulness and meditation. Incorporate these practices into your study routine. By cultivating mindfulness and developing a regular meditation practice, you can deepen your understanding of the scriptures and experience their transformative power firsthand.

- **Engage in Contemplative Inquiry**: Buddhist scriptures often present paradoxes and profound philosophical questions. Engage in contemplative inquiry by reflecting deeply on these teachings. Ask yourself questions, challenge your assumptions, and explore the deeper meanings behind the words. This process of inquiry can lead to personal insights and a deeper understanding of the scriptures.

- **Apply the Teachings in Daily Life**: Ultimately, the purpose of studying Buddhist scriptures is not just intellectual understanding but practical application. Apply the teachings in your daily life by embodying compassion, practicing mindfulness, and cultivating wisdom. This integration of the teachings into your life will deepen your understanding and bring about positive transformation.

Remember, studying Buddhist scriptures is a lifelong journey and shouldn't be rushed. You should approach it with patience, humility, and a willingness to continually learn and grow.

CHAPTER 11

Buddhist Festivals and Celebrations

Buddhism is celebrated through various festivals and celebrations around the world. These events hold great significance for Buddhists, as they commemorate important milestones in the life of the Buddha, honor revered Buddhist figures, and provide opportunities for spiritual reflection and community engagement.

In this chapter, we will delve into some of the major festivals and celebrations in Buddhism, exploring their origins, rituals, and the meanings they hold for practicing Buddhists.

Vesak (Buddha Purnima)

Vesak, also known as Buddha Purnima or Buddha Day, is one of the most significant festivals in Buddhism. The festival is celebrated with great enthusiasm and reverence in Buddhist communities worldwide. The cultural significance of Vesak lies in its commemoration of the birth, enlightenment, and death of the Buddha. It serves as a unifying event that brings together people from different Buddhist traditions and cultures to honor the life and teachings of the Buddha.

Vesak highlights the universal values of compassion, wisdom, and mindfulness, transcending cultural boundaries and fostering a sense of shared humanity.

Celebrated on the full moon day of the Vesak month (usually in May), Vesak is observed with great reverence and joy by Buddhists worldwide. Devotees engage in acts of generosity, practice meditation, and visit temples to offer prayers and make offerings. The festival serves as a reminder of the Buddha's teachings on compassion, wisdom, and the path to liberation.

Asalha Puja (Dharma Day)

Asalha Puja, also known as Dharma Day, is celebrated on the full moon day of the eighth lunar month (usually in July). This festival commemorates the Buddha's first sermon, known as the Dhammacakkappavattana Sutta, in which he expounded the Four Noble Truths and the Eightfold Path.

Asalha Puja holds cultural and spiritual significance as it commemorates the Buddha's first sermon, which laid the foundation for the entire Buddhist tradition. This festival emphasizes the importance of the Dharma, the teachings of the Buddha, and its transformative power in the lives of Buddhists.

Culturally, Asalha Puja is an occasion for Buddhists to come together, listen to sermons, engage in meditation, and make offerings to the monastic community. It reinforces the cultural values of respect for the monastic Sangha and the pursuit of spiritual growth.

Buddhists gather at temples to listen to sermons, engage in meditation, and make offerings to the monastic community.

Kathina Ceremony

The Kathina Ceremony is deeply rooted in Buddhist communities. It is an opportunity for Buddhists to express their gratitude and support for the monastic Sangha. The act of offering robes and other requisites to the monks and nuns reflects the cultural value of generosity and communal harmony.

The Kathina Ceremony also strengthens the bond between the monastic community and practicing Buddhists, fostering a sense of shared responsibility in upholding the teachings.

This significant event takes place after the end of the Vassa, the three-month monastic retreat period, and is an opportunity for people to express their devotion, generosity, and commitment to the monastic Sangha. It is a time of joyous celebration, marked by communal activities, chanting, and meditation.

Uposatha Observance

Uposatha, also known as the Observance Day, is observed on the full moon, new moon, and quarter moon days of each lunar month. On these days, Buddhists engage in heightened spiritual practice, following the Eight Precepts or the Five Precepts more strictly. They visit temples, participate in meditation sessions, listen to Dharma talks, and engage in acts of generosity.

Uposatha Observance holds both cultural and spiritual significance in Buddhist communities. Culturally, it provides a regular rhythm to the lives of Buddhists, reminding them of the importance of ethical conduct and spiritual practice.

The observance of Uposatha days reflects the cultural value of self-discipline, mindfulness, and the pursuit of inner peace. Spiritually, Uposatha Observance offers an opportunity for people to deepen their commitment to the Eight Precepts or the Five Precepts, developing wholesome qualities and purifying the mind.

Wesak Lantern Festival

The Wesak Lantern Festival, celebrated in countries such as Sri Lanka, Malaysia, and Singapore, is a vibrant and visually stunning event held during Vesak.

This festival is a cultural celebration that adds vibrancy and visual splendor to the commemoration of Vesak. Culturally, this festival showcases the artistic talents and creativity of Buddhist communities. It also fosters a sense of unity and joy as people come together to participate in processions, cultural performances, and acts of charity.

Devotees create intricate lanterns, often in the shape of lotus flowers or Buddhist symbols and illuminate them with candles. These lanterns symbolize the light of wisdom and compassion that the Buddha's teachings bring to the world.

Obon Festival

The Obon Festival is deeply rooted in Japanese traditions and customs. It provides an opportunity for families to come together, pay respects to their deceased ancestors, and express gratitude for their contributions. Spiritually, the Obon Festival reminds Buddhists of the impermanence of life and the interconnectedness of past, present, and future generations.

According to Buddhist belief, during this festival, the spirits of the departed return to visit their living relatives. Families clean and decorate graves, offer food and incense, and perform traditional dances called Bon Odori.

The Obon Festival is a time of reflection, gratitude, and the strengthening of family bonds.

Poya Days

Poya Days are monthly observances in Sri Lanka that coincide with the full moon. Each Poya Day commemorates significant events in the life of the Buddha or important moments in Buddhist history. On these days, Buddhists engage in religious activities such as visiting temples, observing precepts, and participating in meditation retreats.

Spiritually, Poya Days offer an opportunity for practitioners to deepen their spiritual practice, reflect on the Buddha's teachings, and cultivate wholesome qualities.

The major festivals and celebrations in Buddhism offer communities a chance to come together, express devotion, and deepen their understanding of the Buddha's teachings. These events serve as reminders of the core principles of Buddhism, such as compassion, wisdom, ethical conduct, and the path to liberation.

By participating in these festivals, Buddhists not only honor the historical milestones of the tradition but also find inspiration and guidance for their own spiritual journeys. Whether it is Vesak, Asalha Puja, the Kathina Ceremony, or other celebrations, these festivals provide a sense of unity, joy, and connection to the teachings of the Buddha.

Participating In and Appreciating Buddhist Festivals

Participating in Buddhists festivals is a wonderful way to immerse ourselves in the vibrant cultural and spiritual traditions of Buddhism. These festivals offer a unique opportunity to engage with the teachings of the Buddha, connect with the Buddhist community, and deepen our understanding of the path to liberation.

So, how can you actively participate in and appreciate Buddhist festivals?

- **Learn about the Festival:** Before participating in a Buddhist festival, take the time to learn about its significance, rituals, and cultural practices. Read books, watch documentaries, or seek guidance from knowledgeable practitioners or teachers. Understanding the historical and spiritual context of the festival will enhance your appreciation and enable you to engage more meaningfully.

- **Attend Temple Celebrations:** Temples play a central role in Buddhist festivals, serving as gathering places for the community. Visit local temples during festival times to witness the vibrant atmosphere, observe rituals, and participate in communal activities. Temples often organize special ceremonies, chanting sessions, and Dharma talks during festivals, providing opportunities for learning and spiritual growth.

- **Engage in Rituals and Offerings:** Buddhist festivals involve various rituals and offerings that hold deep symbolic meaning. Participate in these rituals with respect and mindfulness. Offer flowers, incense, and candles as a gesture of reverence. Take part in prostrations, circumambulations, or other traditional practices, immersing yourself in the collective energy of devotion and spiritual connection.

- **Practice Generosity:** Generosity is a core value in Buddhism, and festivals provide an ideal occasion to practice it. Engage in acts of giving, such as making donations to temples or charitable organizations, offering food to monks or nuns, or supporting community projects. By practicing generosity, you increase your level of compassion and contribute to the well-being of others, aligning with the spirit of the festival.

- **Observe Precepts:** Buddhist festivals often emphasize ethical conduct and mindfulness. Consider observing the Five Precepts or the Eight Precepts during festival times as a way to deepen your spiritual practice. These precepts guide practitioners to abstain from harming living beings, stealing, engaging in sexual misconduct, lying, and consuming intoxicants. By observing the precepts, you create a conducive environment for inner peace and spiritual growth.

- **Engage in Meditation and Reflection:** Festivals provide an opportunity for introspection and contemplation. Set aside time for meditation, either individually or as part of group sessions organized during the festival. Reflect on the teachings of the Buddha, contemplate the impermanence of life, and cultivate gratitude for the opportunity to engage in spiritual practice. Use this time to deepen your understanding of the Dharma and its relevance to your own life.

- **Embrace Cultural Expressions:** Buddhist festivals are often accompanied by cultural expressions such as music, dance, art, and traditional attire. Embrace these cultural elements as a way to connect with the local community and appreciate the diversity within Buddhism. Attend cultural performances, learn traditional dances, or try your hand at creating Buddhist-inspired art.

- **Foster Community Connections:** Buddhist festivals are occasions for building and strengthening community bonds. Engage in conversations with fellow practitioners, share experiences, and learn from one another. Participate in group activities, volunteer for festival preparations, or join study groups or meditation retreats organized during festival times.

Participating in and appreciating Buddhist festivals is a transformative experience that allows you to connect with the teachings of the Buddha, deepen your spiritual practice, and foster a sense of belonging within the Buddhist community.

By immersing yourself in the rituals, practices, and cultural expressions of these festivals, you gain a greater understanding of the core principles of Buddhism and their relevance to your own life.

CHAPTER 12

Buddhism in the Modern World

Buddhism offers insights and practices that can be highly relevant in navigating the complexities of today's fast-paced society. In a world marked by rapid technological advancements, social and environmental challenges, and increasing levels of stress and disconnection, Buddhism provides a framework for personal transformation and societal well-being.

Let's delve deeper into the relevance of Buddhism in contemporary society, examining its teachings, practices, and values that can contribute to individual and collective benefits.

- **Mindfulness in the Digital Age**: In the age of constant distractions and information overload, the practice of mindfulness becomes increasingly relevant. Mindfulness helps us develop present-moment awareness, allowing a deeper understanding of our thoughts, emotions, and actions. By practicing mindfulness, we can navigate the digital landscape with greater intentionality, reducing stress, enhancing focus, and fostering healthier relationships with technology.

- **Compassion and Social Engagement**: Buddhism's emphasis on compassion and social engagement is highly relevant in addressing the social and environmental challenges of contemporary society. The Buddhist concept of "Bodhisattva," one who seeks enlightenment for the benefit of all beings, inspires us to extend our compassion beyond personal well-being. Engaging in acts of kindness, volunteering, and advocating for social justice aligns with Buddhist values and contributes to creating a more compassionate and equitable society.

- **Ethical Conduct and Environmental Stewardship**: Buddhism's ethical framework, encapsulated in the Five Precepts, provides guidance for responsible and sustainable living. The precepts, which include refraining from harming living beings and practicing mindful consumption, are highly relevant in addressing environmental issues such as climate change and biodiversity loss. By adopting a mindful and ethical approach to consumption, we can reduce our ecological footprint and contribute to the well-being of the planet.

- **Psychological Well-being and Mental Health**: As we grapple with increasing levels of stress, anxiety, and mental health challenges, Buddhism offers valuable insights and practices for cultivating psychological well-being. Meditation, mindfulness-based stress reduction (MBSR), and loving-kindness practices have been shown to reduce stress, improve emotional regulation, and enhance overall mental well-being. Integrating these practices into daily life can support us in navigating the pressures of modern society.

- **Embracing Impermanence and Cultivating Resilience**: Buddhism's teachings on impermanence and non-attachment provide a valuable perspective in a world characterized by constant change and uncertainty. By recognizing the impermanent nature of all things, we can develop resilience and adaptability in the face of challenges. Buddhism encourages us to let go of attachments to outcomes and embrace the present moment, fostering a sense of peace and calmness in the middle of life's ups and downs.

- **Interconnectedness and Global Citizenship**: Buddhism's teachings on interconnectedness and interdependence resonate deeply in an increasingly globalized world. The recognition that all beings are interconnected encourages us to cultivate a sense of global citizenship and responsibility. By embracing the principles of non-harming and compassion, we can contribute to the well-being of not only our immediate communities but also the global community at large.

- **Wisdom and Critical Thinking**: Buddhism places great emphasis on wisdom and discernment, encouraging us to question and investigate the nature of reality. In a world inundated with information and misinformation, wisdom and critical thinking is crucial. Buddhist teachings on impermanence, emptiness, and the nature of suffering provide a framework for deep inquiry and reflection, enabling us to navigate the complexities of contemporary society with clarity and discernment.

As you can see, Buddhism's teachings and practices are very relevant in today's society. From mindfulness and compassion to ethical conduct and environmental stewardship, Buddhism provides a holistic framework for personal and societal well-being.

Exploring the Integration of Buddhist Principles in Various Fields

Buddhist principles, with an emphasis on mindfulness, compassion, and wisdom, have found resonance beyond traditional religious contexts. The integration of Buddhist principles in various fields, such as psychology, education, healthcare, and leadership, has gained recognition for their potential to enhance well-being, foster ethical conduct, and promote positive change.

Let's explore how Buddhist principles are being integrated into these fields, highlighting their transformative impact and relevance in modern society.

- **Psychology and Mindfulness:** The integration of mindfulness has gained significant attention in psychology. Interventions such as Mindfulness-Based Stress Reduction (MBSR) and Mindfulness-Based Cognitive Therapy (MBCT), have been developed and widely adopted in the field. These practices help us cultivate present-moment awareness, reduce stress, manage emotions, and enhance overall psychological well-being. The integration of mindfulness in psychotherapy has shown promising results in treating various mental health conditions, including depression, anxiety, and addiction.

- **Education and Social-Emotional Learning:** Buddhist principles have also found their way into the field of education, particularly in the realm of social-emotional learning (SEL). SEL programs incorporate mindfulness practices, empathy training, and ethical values to foster emotional intelligence, resilience, and positive relationships among students. By integrating Buddhist principles into education, schools are creating nurturing environments that support the holistic development of students, promoting their well-being and academic success.

- **Healthcare and Mind-Body Medicine:** Buddhist principles have influenced the field of healthcare through the integration of mind-body medicine approaches. Practices such as meditation, yoga, and tai chi, rooted in Buddhist traditions, are increasingly recognized for their therapeutic benefits. These practices have been shown to reduce stress, improve immune function, and enhance overall physical and mental well-being. Integrative medicine programs in healthcare settings are incorporating these practices to complement conventional treatments and promote holistic healing.

- **Leadership and Ethical Conduct:** Buddhist principles offer valuable insights for ethical leadership in various domains. The emphasis on compassion, wisdom, and non-harming can guide leaders to make decisions that prioritize the well-being of individuals and communities. Mindful leadership practices, such as self-reflection, active listening, and empathy, are being integrated into leadership development programs. These practices foster ethical conduct, enhance interpersonal relationships, and promote sustainable and compassionate leadership.

- **Environmental Sustainability and Engaged Buddhism:** Engaged Buddhism, a movement that integrates Buddhist principles with social and environmental activism, addresses the urgent need for environmental sustainability. Buddhist teachings on interconnectedness and non-harming inspire us to take action to protect the environment. Engaged Buddhist organizations and initiatives promote sustainable practices, environmental education, and advocacy for ecological justice.

- **Conflict Resolution and Peacebuilding:** Buddhist principles offer valuable insights for conflict resolution and peacebuilding efforts. The practice of mindfulness cultivates self-awareness and emotional regulation, enabling us to respond to conflicts with compassion and non-violence. They also provide a foundation for understanding the root causes of conflicts and promoting reconciliation. Mindfulness-based conflict resolution programs are being implemented in various settings, fostering dialogue, empathy, and sustainable peace.

- **Business and Ethical Practices:** Buddhist principles are increasingly being integrated into the business world to promote ethical practices and conscious capitalism. Mindfulness practices are being incorporated into workplace settings to enhance employee well-being, productivity, and job satisfaction. Ethical business models inspired by Buddhist principles prioritize social and environmental responsibility, fair trade, and sustainable practices. By integrating Buddhist principles into business, organizations are fostering a more compassionate and sustainable approach to economic growth.

The integration of Buddhist principles in various fields demonstrates their relevance and transformative potential in today's digital world. Buddhist principles offer valuable insights and practices that enhance well-being, foster ethical conduct, and promote positive change.

Addressing Challenges and Misconceptions About Buddhism

Buddhism has faced various challenges and misconceptions throughout its existence. These challenges range from cultural misunderstandings to misinterpretations of Buddhist teachings. Addressing these challenges and misconceptions is crucial for fostering a more accurate understanding of Buddhism and promoting intercultural dialogue.

Let's discuss some challenges and misconceptions about Buddhism and provide insights to address them.

- **Cultural Appropriation:** One challenge Buddhism faces is cultural appropriation, where aspects of Buddhist practices and symbols are taken out of their original context and used inappropriately. It is important to respect the cultural and religious significance of Buddhist traditions and symbols, as with all other religions too. Engaging in sincere study, seeking guidance from knowledgeable practitioners, and approaching Buddhist practices with humility and respect can help address this challenge.

- **Misinterpretation of Concepts:** Buddhist concepts, such as karma, rebirth, and emptiness, are often misunderstood or misinterpreted. These concepts require careful study and contemplation to grasp their deeper meanings. Seeking guidance from qualified teachers, studying authentic Buddhist texts, and engaging in open-minded dialogue can help overcome misconceptions and foster a more accurate understanding of these concepts.

- **Simplification and Commercialization:** In contemporary society, there is a tendency to simplify and commercialize Buddhist teachings, reducing them to self-help techniques or trendy lifestyle choices. This oversimplification can dilute the profound wisdom and transformative potential of Buddhism. It is important to engage in in-depth study, practice, and reflection, recognizing that Buddhism offers a comprehensive path to liberation rather than quick fixes or superficial trends.

- **Misrepresentation of Meditation:** Meditation is often associated solely with relaxation or stress reduction, overlooking its deeper purpose in Buddhism. Meditation is a practice that encourages mindfulness, concentration, and insight, leading to profound personal transformation. Educating others about the multifaceted nature of meditation and its role within the broader context of Buddhist practice can help correct this misconception.

- **Gender Equality:** Buddhism, like many religious traditions, has faced challenges regarding gender equality. Historical and cultural factors have led to the marginalization of women in certain Buddhist communities. However, it is important to recognize that Buddhism itself does not inherently promote gender inequality. Many Buddhist teachings emphasize the inherent worth and potential for awakening in all beings, regardless of gender. Encouraging inclusive practices, supporting female monastic communities, and promoting gender equality within Buddhist institutions can help overcome this issue.

- **Violence and Extremism:** While Buddhism promotes non-violence and compassion, it is not immune to the influence of human actions and historical contexts. Instances of violence or extremism associated with Buddhism should be understood as deviations from the core teachings. Emphasizing the importance of ethical conduct, compassion, and non-harming can help overcome these misconceptions.

- **Cultural and Regional Diversity:** Buddhism encompasses a wide range of cultural and regional expressions, leading to misconceptions that assume a single Buddhist identity. It is important to recognize and appreciate the diversity within Buddhism, including Theravada, Mahayana, and Vajrayana traditions, as well as the various cultural adaptations across different countries. Engaging in intercultural dialogue, studying the history and development of Buddhist traditions, and fostering respect for diverse expressions of Buddhism addresses this falsehood.

By addressing these challenges and misconceptions, we can promote intercultural dialogue, cultivate mutual respect, and foster a more accurate and inclusive understanding of Buddhism in contemporary society.

Chapter 13

Engaging with Buddhist Communities

Finding and connecting with local Buddhist communities can be a rewarding and enriching experience for anyone interested in exploring Buddhism or deepening their practice. Engaging with a community provides opportunities for learning, support, and the development of spiritual friendships.

Of course, understanding how to find and connect with local Buddhist communities can be difficult, so let's discuss how to do that in this chapter.

- **Research and Online Resources:** Start by doing some research to identify Buddhist communities in your local area. Online resources such as directories, forums, and social media groups can be valuable tools for finding nearby Buddhist centers, temples, or meditation groups. Websites like Buddhanet.net, DharmaNet.org, or Meetup.com often provide comprehensive listings of Buddhist organizations and events. Explore these resources to gather information about the different traditions, practices, and activities available in your area.

- **Visit Local Buddhist Centers and Temples:** One of the most direct ways to connect with a local Buddhist community is to visit nearby Buddhist centers or temples. Many centers offer regular meditation sessions, Dharma talks, and other activities that are open to the public. Take the opportunity to attend these events, observe the practices, and engage in conversations with the community members. This will allow you to get a sense of the community's atmosphere, teachings, and values.

- **Attend Retreats and Workshops:** Retreats and workshops provide immersive experiences and opportunities to connect with like-minded individuals. Look for retreats or workshops organized by local Buddhist communities or renowned teachers in your area. These events often offer a structured program of meditation, teachings, and discussions, allowing you to deepen your understanding of Buddhism and connect with fellow practitioners on a more profound level.

- **Seek Guidance from Teachers and Practitioners:** Teachers and experienced practitioners can provide valuable guidance and support on your Buddhist journey. If you resonate with a particular teacher or practitioner, reach out to them for guidance or inquire about any study groups or practice sessions they may lead. Establishing a mentor-student relationship or participating in study groups can offer a more personalized and focused learning experience.

- **Engage in Volunteer Activities:** Many Buddhist communities engage in volunteer activities as a way to serve others and practice generosity. Participating in volunteer work can be an excellent way to connect with the community, contribute to meaningful causes, and deepen your understanding of Buddhist values in action.

- **Attend Festivals and Celebrations:** Buddhist festivals and celebrations provide opportunities to connect with the wider Buddhist community and experience the richness of Buddhist traditions. Attend local Vesak celebrations, Dharma Day events, or other Buddhist festivals in your area. These events often include cultural performances, rituals, and communal activities that foster a sense of unity and joy.

- **Join Online Buddhist Communities:** In addition to local connections, online Buddhist communities can provide a platform for learning, discussion, and support. Join online forums, social media groups, or virtual meditation groups to connect with practitioners from around the world. Engaging in online communities can be particularly beneficial if you live in an area with limited access to local Buddhist communities. However, it is important to balance online engagement with in-person connections to fully experience the richness of Buddhist practice.

- **Encourage Mindful Relationships:** Connecting with a local Buddhist community is not just about attending events or participating in activities. It is also about cultivating mindful relationships with fellow Buddhists. Take the time to engage in conversations, listen deeply, and share your own experiences. Attend social gatherings or community meals to foster connections beyond formal practice settings. Building meaningful relationships within the community can provide support, inspiration, and a sense of belonging on your Buddhist path.

- **Respect Cultural Differences:** When connecting with a local Buddhist community, it is essential to respect and appreciate cultural differences. Buddhism is a diverse tradition with various cultural expressions and practices. Be open-minded, curious, and respectful of different customs, rituals, and traditions. Embrace the opportunity to learn from different Buddhist cultures and deepen your understanding of the universality of Buddhist teachings.

- **Be Patient and Open to Growth:** This is a journey that requires patience, openness, and a willingness to grow. It takes time to find a community that resonates with your values and aspirations. Be open to exploring different traditions, practices, and teachings. Embrace the challenges and opportunities for growth that arise in the process of connecting with a community.

Finding and connecting with local Buddhist communities is a valuable step in deepening your understanding and practice of

Buddhism. Through research, visits to local centers, attending retreats, seeking guidance, engaging in volunteer activities, participating in festivals, and cultivating mindful relationships, you can establish connections that support your spiritual journey.

Remember to approach these connections with an open mind, respect for cultural differences, and a willingness to learn and grow.

Understanding the Role of Sangha (Spiritual Community) in Buddhism

The Sangha plays a vital role in supporting and nurturing the spiritual growth and well-being of Buddhists. Let's explore the significance of the Sangha in Buddhism and the benefits it offers to individuals and the wider community.

As we've already explored, the term "Sangha" refers to the community of Buddhist practitioners, including monastics and laypeople, who come together to support each other on the path to awakening. The Sangha has its roots in the early Buddhist tradition, where the Buddha established a community of monastic disciples who dedicated their lives to the practice and propagation of the Dharma.

The Sangha provides a supportive environment for people to deepen their practice and cultivate spiritual friendships. Practicing alongside like-minded individuals who share similar aspirations creates a sense of camaraderie and mutual support. The Sangha offers a space for us to share experiences, seek guidance, and receive encouragement on our spiritual journey.

In addition, the Sangha plays a crucial role in preserving and transmitting the teachings of the Buddha, known as the Dharma. Monastics, who have dedicated their lives to the study and practice of the Dharma, serve as custodians of the teachings. Through their study, contemplation, and realization, they ensure the continuity and authenticity of the Dharma for future generations.

The Sangha serves as a living embodiment of Buddhist values and principles. Monastics, through their renunciation and commitment to ethical conduct, inspire Buddhists to cultivate virtues such as compassion, generosity, and mindfulness. The Sangha provides a model for individuals to observe and learn from, encouraging the integration of Buddhist teachings into daily life.

Of course, the Sangha plays a central role in conducting rituals and ceremonies that mark important milestones in the lives of Buddhists. These rituals, such as ordinations, weddings, and funerals, provide opportunities for the community to come together, offer support, and celebrate or commemorate significant events. The Sangha's presence and participation in these rituals lend them a spiritual dimension and reinforce the interconnectedness of the community.

Monastics and lay practitioners alike also participate in charitable activities, such as providing food, healthcare, and education to those in need. Engaging in acts of service not only benefits the wider community but also cultivates compassion, generosity, and selflessness within the Sangha.

At the same time, the Sangha provides opportunities for people to attend intensive meditation retreats and group practice. Retreats offer a supportive environment for deepening meditation practice, cultivating mindfulness, and experiencing the transformative power of sustained contemplative practice. Practicing together in a retreat setting strengthens the collective energy and supports individual progress.

Overall, the Sangha fosters a sense of community and connection among local Buddhists. Regular gatherings, such as meditation sessions, Dharma discussions, or social events, provide opportunities for people to come together, share their practice, and build meaningful relationships. The Sangha offers a sense of belonging and support, particularly for those seeking spiritual companionship in a world that can feel disconnected.

Participating in Group Practices and Activities

Whether it is meditation sessions, Dharma discussions, retreats, or service projects, group activities offer unique opportunities for learning, support, and growth. In this section, let's explore the benefits of participating in group practices and activities and understand how to make the most of these experiences.

- **Collective Energy and Support:** Group practices harness the collective energy of like-minded individuals, creating a supportive and inspiring environment. Meditating or engaging in spiritual activities together can deepen our own practice through the shared focus and intention. The presence of others can provide motivation, accountability, and a sense of belonging, especially during challenging times. The collective energy of the group can uplift and sustain our efforts, fostering a deeper connection to the practice.

- **Learning from Others:** Group practices offer opportunities to learn from the experiences and insights of fellow practitioners. Dharma discussions, study groups, or retreats provide platforms for sharing perspectives, asking questions, and engaging in meaningful dialogue. By listening to others' perspectives and reflections, we can gain new insights, broaden our understanding, and deepen our own practice. Learning from others' experiences can inspire and guide our own spiritual journey.

- **Boosting Compassion and Interconnectedness:** Group practices provide a space to cultivate compassion and develop a sense of interconnectedness. Engaging in service projects or acts of kindness as a group fosters a collective spirit of generosity and care. By working together to alleviate suffering and support others, we develop empathy, compassion, and a deeper understanding of the interdependence of all beings. Group activities can be transformative, fostering a sense of unity and shared purpose.

- **Deepening Concentration and Mindfulness:** Participating in group meditation sessions or retreats can deepen our concentration and mindfulness practice. The collective energy and focused atmosphere of a group setting can support the development of sustained attention and present-moment awareness. Meditating together can create a sense of shared stillness and enhance the depth of our own practice. Group retreats, in particular, provide an immersive experience that allows for sustained practice and deepening insight.

- **Cultivating Spiritual Friendship:** Group practices offer opportunities to cultivate spiritual friendships, or kalyana-mittata. These friendships provide a sense of camaraderie, understanding, and encouragement on our spiritual path. Engaging in group activities allows for the development of meaningful connections with like-minded individuals who can offer support, guidance, and inspiration. Spiritual friendships can be a source of strength and companionship.

- **Expanding Perspectives:** Participating in group practices exposes us to a diverse range of perspectives and approaches to spirituality. Within a spiritual community, there may be practitioners from different backgrounds, traditions, and levels of experience. Engaging with this diversity can broaden our understanding, challenge preconceived notions, and foster a more inclusive and open-minded approach to spirituality.

- **Deepening Ethical Conduct:** Group practices provide an opportunity to reinforce ethical conduct. Engaging in activities with a community that upholds shared values and ethical guidelines supports the development of virtuous qualities. Practicing together encourages accountability and the cultivation of integrity, kindness, and mindfulness in our actions. The collective commitment to ethical conduct strengthens our resolve and fosters a supportive environment for personal growth.

- **Nurturing a Sense of Gratitude:** Participating in group practices and activities can create a sense of gratitude for the opportunity to engage with a spiritual community. Recognizing the support, guidance, and inspiration received from the group fosters a deep appreciation for the collective effort and the teachings that have been passed down through generations. Gratitude nourishes humility, contentment, and a sense of interconnectedness, enhancing our spiritual journey.

Tips for Making the Most of Group Practices and Activities:

1. Approach group activities with an open mind and a willingness to learn from others.
2. Engage actively by participating in discussions, asking questions, and sharing your own insights and experiences.
3. Be respectful of others' perspectives and create a safe and inclusive space for dialogue.
4. Embrace challenges and discomfort as opportunities for growth and self-reflection.
5. Practice deep listening and cultivate empathy towards others' experiences and struggles.
6. Offer support and encouragement to fellow practitioners, fostering a sense of community and interconnectedness.
7. Reflect on your experiences after group activities, integrating the insights gained into your personal practice and daily life.

8. Maintain a regular personal practice alongside group activities to deepen your understanding and cultivate self-reliance.

Participating in group practices and activities within a spiritual community offers numerous benefits for personal growth, support, and learning. The collective energy, shared experiences, and diverse perspectives found in group settings can deepen our practice, foster compassion, and nurture a sense of interconnectedness.

Chapter 14

Creating Your Own Buddhist Practice

Creating a personal Buddhist practice that suits your lifestyle is a meaningful and transformative endeavor. Buddhism offers a flexible framework that can be adapted to various lifestyles, allowing us to integrate its teachings and practices into our daily lives.

However, creating a personal Buddhist practice that aligns with your unique needs, interests, and schedule takes time. Let's take a deeper look at the steps to do it.

- **Clarify Your Intentions:** Begin by clarifying your intentions. Reflect on what draws you to Buddhism and what you hope to gain from your practice. Whether it is focusing on mindfulness, developing compassion, or seeking liberation from suffering, having a clear intention will guide your choices and help you stay focused.

- **Study and Learn:** Engage in study to deepen your understanding of Buddhist teachings. Read books, listen to Dharma talks, and explore online resources to gain knowledge about the core principles and practices of Buddhism. Familiarize yourself with different Buddhist traditions and teachings to find what resonates with you. This study will provide a foundation for your personal practice.

- **Choose Core Practices:** Identify the core practices that you would like to incorporate into your personal Buddhist practice. These practices may include meditation, mindfulness, chanting, or recitation of sutras. Start with one or two practices that resonate with you and gradually expand as you become more comfortable. Experiment with different techniques to find what works best for you.

- **Establish a Routine:** Create a routine that allows for regular engagement with your Buddhist practice. Consider your daily schedule and find a time that works best for you. It could be early morning, during a lunch break, or in the evening. Consistency is key, so aim for a realistic and sustainable routine that you can commit to. Start with shorter sessions and gradually increase the duration as your practice deepens.

- **Create a Sacred Space:** Designate a space in your home as a sacred space for your Buddhist practice. It could be a corner of a room, a small altar, or a cushion where you can sit in meditation. Personalize this space with objects that inspire and remind you of your practice, such as statues, candles, or meaningful symbols. This dedicated space will serve as a visual reminder of your commitment to your Buddhist practice.

- **Integrate Mindfulness into Daily Activities:** Bring mindfulness into your daily activities by cultivating present-moment awareness. Whether you are eating, walking, or engaging in routine tasks, practice being fully present and attentive. Use these moments as opportunities to cultivate mindfulness, observe your thoughts and emotions, and bring a sense of mindfulness into your daily life.

- **Seek Community and Support:** Connect with like-minded individuals and seek support from a Buddhist community. Join local meditation groups, attend retreats, or participate in online forums to engage with others on the Buddhist path. Sharing experiences, discussing teachings, and receiving guidance from experienced practitioners can provide valuable support and inspiration.

- **Reflect and Journal:** Take time to reflect on your practice and journal about your experiences. Reflect on the insights gained, challenges encountered, and progress made. Journaling can help deepen your understanding, clarify your thoughts, and track your growth over time. It also serves as a record of your personal journey and can be a source of inspiration in the future.

- **Adapt to Changing Circumstances:** Recognize that your personal Buddhist practice may need to adapt to changing circumstances. Life is dynamic, and your practice should be flexible enough to accommodate different phases and challenges. Be open to adjusting your routine, practices, and intentions as needed. Embrace impermanence and view changes as opportunities for growth and adaptation.

- **Be Patient and Compassionate:** Remember that establishing a personal Buddhist practice is a lifelong journey. Focus on patience and compassion toward yourself as you navigate the ups and downs of your practice. Be gentle and forgiving when facing obstacles or distractions. Approach your practice with a sense of curiosity, openness, and non-judgment.

Creating a personal Buddhist practice that suits your lifestyle is a deeply personal and transformative process. There is no one size fits all answer here, but by taking your time and focusing on yourself, you can develop a practice that aligns with your unique needs and supports your spiritual growth.

Setting Goals and Milestones for Your Spiritual Journey

Setting goals and milestones for your spiritual journey is a valuable practice that can provide direction, motivation, and a sense of progress. Just as in any other aspect of life, having clear objectives and milestones can help guide your spiritual growth and deepen your connection to your chosen path.

In this section, we will explore the importance of setting goals and milestones for your spiritual journey and provide guidance on how to approach this process.

- **Reflect on Your Values:** Consider your core values and how they align with your spiritual aspirations. Identify the values that are most important to you and how they can guide your goals. For example, if compassion is a core value, you may set a goal to engage in regular acts of kindness or to deepen your understanding of compassion through study and practice.

- **Set Specific and Realistic Goals:** Set specific and realistic goals that are aligned with your intentions and values. Break down your larger aspirations into smaller, achievable steps. For example, if your intention is to deepen your meditation practice, you may set a goal to meditate for a specific duration each day or to attend a meditation retreat within a certain timeframe.

- **Focus on Process Goals:** While outcome-oriented goals can be motivating, it is important to also focus on process goals. Process goals are centered around the actions and practices that lead to growth and transformation. For example, instead of setting a goal to achieve a specific level of spiritual insight, you may set a process goal to engage in daily mindfulness practice or to study a particular text.

- **Create a Timeline:** Establish a timeline for your goals and milestones. Consider both short-term and long-term objectives. Short-term goals can provide a sense of immediate progress and keep you motivated, while long-term goals provide a broader vision for your spiritual journey. Be flexible with your timeline, allowing for adjustments and adaptations as needed.

- **Track Your Progress:** Regularly assess and track your progress towards your goals and milestones. This can be done through journaling, self-reflection, or discussions with a mentor or spiritual friend. Celebrate your achievements and acknowledge the growth you have experienced. If you encounter challenges or setbacks, use them as opportunities for learning and adjust your course.

- **Seek Guidance and Support:** Engage with a mentor, teacher, or spiritual community to seek guidance and support in setting and achieving your goals. They can offer insights, accountability, and encouragement along your journey. Share your goals with them and seek their feedback and guidance on how to best approach your spiritual aspirations.

- **Embrace Flexibility and Adaptation:** Recognize that your spiritual journey is dynamic and subject to change. Be open to adapting your goals and milestones as you grow and evolve. Allow for new insights, experiences, and teachings to shape your path. Embrace the fluidity of your journey and be willing to let go of goals that no longer serve your growth.

- **Celebrate Milestones and Reflect:** When you reach a milestone or achieve a goal, take the time to celebrate and acknowledge your progress. Reflect on the growth you have experienced, and the lessons learned along the way. Use these moments of reflection to refine your goals, set new ones, and deepen your commitment to your spiritual journey.

Setting goals and milestones for your spiritual journey can provide direction, motivation, and a sense of progress. Your goals must be yours and yours alone. With time and effort, you can create a framework that supports your spiritual growth and deepens your connection to your chosen path.

Resources and Further Study for Deepening Your Understanding of Buddhism

Deepening your understanding of Buddhism is a lifelong journey that requires continuous learning and exploration. Fortunately, there are numerous resources available to support your study and provide insights into the teachings and practices of Buddhism.

- **Sacred Texts and Sutras:** Buddhism has a vast collection of sacred texts and sutras that contain the teachings of the Buddha and his disciples. The Tripitaka, also known as the Pali Canon, is the foundational scripture in Theravada Buddhism. The Mahayana tradition has its own collection of sutras, such as the Lotus Sutra, Heart Sutra, and Diamond Sutra. Reading and studying these texts can provide a direct source of wisdom and insight into Buddhist philosophy and practice.

- **Commentaries and Translations:** To aid in understanding the sacred texts, commentaries and translations by renowned Buddhist scholars can be invaluable. These works provide explanations, interpretations, and contextual information that shed light on the teachings. Some notable scholars include Thich Nhat Hanh, Bhikkhu Bodhi, and Geshe Kelsang Gyatso. Seek out their commentaries and translations to deepen your understanding of Buddhist texts.

- **Online Courses and Study Programs:** Online courses and study programs offer structured learning experiences that cater to different levels of understanding. Websites like Coursera, edX, and Udemy offer courses on various aspects of Buddhism, including its history, philosophy, and practices. Additionally, many Buddhist organizations and centers provide online study programs that cover a wide range of topics, allowing you to engage with experienced teachers and fellow students.

- **Meditation Retreats and Workshops:** Participating in meditation retreats and workshops can deepen your experiential understanding of Buddhist practices. These immersive experiences provide opportunities to learn from experienced teachers, engage in intensive meditation practice, and receive guidance on various aspects of the path. Retreats and workshops are often offered by Buddhist centers and organizations, both locally and internationally.

- **Dharma Talks and Podcasts:** Dharma talks, given by experienced teachers and practitioners, offer insights into Buddhist teachings and their practical application. Many Buddhist centers and organizations record and share these talks online, making them accessible to a wider audience. Podcasts dedicated to Buddhism, such as "Buddhist Geeks" and "Secular Buddhism," provide a wealth of discussions and interviews with prominent Buddhist teachers and scholars.

- **Buddhist Literature and Biographies:** Buddhist literature, both classical and contemporary, offers a wealth of knowledge and inspiration. Books by renowned Buddhist authors like Thich Nhat Hanh, Pema Chödrön, and Jack Kornfield provide accessible and practical insights into Buddhist philosophy and practice. Biographies of Buddhist masters, such as "The Life of the Buddha" by Bhikkhu Ñanamoli or "The Life of Milarepa" by Tsangnyön Heruka, offer glimpses into the lives of enlightened beings and their spiritual journeys.

- **Engaging with Buddhist Communities:** Engaging with local Buddhist communities and attending their events can provide opportunities for learning and discussion. Participate in meditation sessions, Dharma discussions, or study groups offered by Buddhist centers or temples. Engaging with experienced practitioners and teachers within a community setting can deepen your understanding and provide valuable insights.

- **Mindfulness Apps and Online Resources:** Mindfulness apps and online resources can support your daily practice and provide guidance. Apps like Insight Timer, Calm, and Headspace offer guided meditations, teachings, and timers to support your mindfulness practice. Online resources, such as websites and blogs dedicated to Buddhism, provide articles, teachings, and discussions on various aspects of Buddhism.

- **Interfaith Dialogue and Comparative Religion:** Engaging in interfaith dialogue and exploring comparative religion can provide a broader perspective on Buddhism. Understanding how Buddhism relates to other religious traditions can deepen your understanding of its unique teachings and practices. Interfaith events, conferences, and books on comparative religion can facilitate this exploration.

- **Personal Reflection and Contemplation:** Lastly, personal reflection and contemplation are essential for deepening your understanding of Buddhism. Set aside time for self-reflection, journaling, and contemplation on the teachings and their relevance to your own life. Cultivate a regular meditation practice to develop insight and deepen your connection to the teachings.

There are numerous resources available to support your study and deepen your understanding of Buddhism. Embrace these resources and approaches to continue your journey of learning and growth in the profound wisdom of Buddhism.

Conclusion

Throughout this book, we have explored the core teachings of Buddhism, such as the Four Noble Truths, the Eightfold Path, and the concept of impermanence. We have delved into the practices of meditation, mindfulness, and compassion, understanding their transformative power in cultivating inner peace and wisdom.

We have also examined the historical and cultural context of Buddhism, recognizing its diverse expressions and adaptations across different regions and time periods. This all helps us appreciate the beauty and diversity within Buddhist traditions.

In our journey, we have encountered the lives and teachings of enlightened beings, such as the historical Buddha, Bodhisattvas, and revered masters. Their stories have inspired us and provided guidance on the path to awakening.

We have explored the relevance of Buddhism in contemporary society, recognizing its potential to address the challenges of the modern world. From mindfulness in the digital age to ethical conduct in business, Buddhism offers valuable insights and practices that can guide us towards a more compassionate, mindful, and sustainable way of living.

Throughout this book, we have emphasized the importance of personal practice and the cultivation of a spiritual path that suits our individual needs and circumstances. We have encouraged self-reflection, mindfulness, and the integration of Buddhist principles into our daily lives.

As we conclude this enlightening journey, it is important to remember that the exploration of Buddhism is a lifelong endeavor.

The wisdom and teachings of Buddhism are vast, and our understanding will continue to deepen as we engage in further study, practice, and reflection.

May this book serve as a stepping stone, igniting a lifelong curiosity and commitment to the path of Buddhism. May it inspire you to continue exploring, learning, and integrating the teachings into your own life, fostering inner peace, compassion, and wisdom.

Welcome to the enlightening journey of exploring Buddhism, a path that offers profound insights, transformative practices, and the potential for liberation. May your journey be filled with joy, growth, and the realization of your true nature.

References

"5 Simple Ways to Incorporate Mindfulness into Your Daily Routine." (n.d.). https://www.thewellnysstree.com/blog/5-simple-ways-to-incorporate-mindfulness-into-your-daily-routine

Benefits to acupuncture. (2023, February 9). Loren Stiteler LAc. https://www.stitelermed.com/post/benefits-to-acupuncture

Dharmashop Kamalashila. (n.d.). *Buddhist Beginners - Dharmashop Kamalashila*. https://dharmashop.de/en/product-category/books/buddhistische-einsteiger/

Discoveringasmr. (2022, October 12). *Definition, History, types and benefits • Yoga Basics - DiscoveringASMR*. DiscoveringASMR. https://discoveringasmr.com/2022/10/12/definition-history-types-and-benefits-yoga-basics/

Dreamzandexperiences, & Dreamzandexperiences. (2023, March 29). Ram Navami 2023 - Dreamz&Experiences. *Ram Navami 2023 - Dreamz&Experiences*. https://dreamzandexperiences.com/2023/03/30/ram-navami-2023/

June, P. B. C. O. (2020, June 24). *Birth Chart Guide - Understanding the basics of Astrological natal charts*. Christin Medium. https://www.christin-medium.com/birth-chart

Knight, H. (2023, April 5). *Buddhist Beliefs | Full list & Complete guide*. Faith Inspires. https://faithinspires.org/buddhist-beliefs/

McKnight, J. (2023, August 13). Comparison of ancient and modern meditation practices: Exploring differences and similarities. *Planet Meditate*. https://planetmeditate.com/comparison-ancient-and-modern-meditation/

Mike. (2023, May 25). *Mindful Drinking: A path to Healthier choices and Balanced living*. ABC Business News. https://www.abcbnews.com/mindful-drinking-a-path-to-healthier-choices-and-balanced-living/

OpenLibrary.org. (2009). *Meditation from Buddhist, Hindu, and Taoist perspectives by Robert J. Altobello | Open Library*. Open Library. https://openlibrary.org/books/OL23180788M/Meditation_from_Buddhist_Hindu_and_Taoist_perspectives

Persisting through hard times, chapter 4. (2023, February 2). Live Again: No Matter What - Get Inspired to Follow Your Dreams. https://davidwpaton.com/persisting6/

Rooted In Mindfulness. (n.d.). https://www.rootedinmindfulness.org/glossary-terms/investigation

Subodhgupta. (2022, December 31). *Four Noble Truths of Buddhism Meaning*. Buddha Stories & Teachings | Buddhism. https://www.subodhgupta.com/four-noble-truths-of-buddhism-meaning/

The benefits of mindfulness for stress reduction and improved mental health – Simplify Mindfulness. (2022, December 30). https://simplifymindfulness.com/2022/12/30/the-benefits-of-mindfulness-for-stress-reduction-and-improved-mental-health/

The Four Noble Truths-The Dalai Lama. (n.d.). NepaCrafts Product. https://www.nepacrafts.com/products/the-four-noble-truths-the-dalai-lama

The role of Psychology in Buddhism. (n.d.). https://www.psychbreakthrough.com/breakthrough-blog/the-role-of-psychology-in-buddhism-

There are beings with little dust in their eyes. . .. (2022, June 17). Little Dust Buddhist Community. https://littledust.org/2022/06/17/there-are-beings-with-little-dust-in-their-eyes/

thezensite:A Note On Dharma Transmission And The Institutions Of Zen. (n.d.). http://www.thezensite.com/ZenEssays/CriticalZen/Dharma_Transmission_Institutions.html

References

Waldrop, J. (2022, September 19). *Buddhism and Longtermism are not Mutually Exclusive.* Justin W. Waldrop. https://justinwaldrop.com/buddhism-and-longtermism/

Walking Meditation |. (n.d.). http://spiritualpractice.ca/what/what-2/the-common-christian-practices/meditation/forms-of-meditation/walking-meditation/

What is hatha yoga? - Yoga kawa. (n.d.). Yoga Kawa. https://www.yogakawa.com/blog/hatha-yoga/

Winny, K. (2019, June 14). 5 ways to start meditating. *katherinewinny.* https://www.katherinewinny.com/single-post/2019/06/14/5-ways-to-start-meditating

Printed in Great Britain
by Amazon